Lost in the Sun

Roy Gleason's Odyssey from the Outfield to the Battlefield

Roy Gleason
as told to Wallace Wasinack
with Mark Langill

www.SportsPublishingLLC.com

ISBN: 1-58261-944-1

Publishers: Peter L. Bannon and Joseph J. Bannon Sr.
Senior managing editor: Susan M. Moyer
Acquisitions editor: Mike Pearson
Developmental editor: Travis W. Moran
Art director: K. Jeffrey Higgerson
Dust jacket design: Joseph Brumleve
Interior layout: Kathryn R. Holleman
Imaging: Kathryn R. Holleman, Dustin Hubbart, and Heidi Norsen
Photo editor: Erin Linden-Levy
Media and promotions managers: Kelley Brown (regional),
    Randy Fouts (national), Maurey Williamson (print)

Printed in the United States of America

Sports Publishing L.L.C.
804 North Neil Street
Champaign, IL 61820

Phone: 1-877-424-2665
Fax: 217-363-2073
www.SportsPublishingLLC.com

Contents

Foreword

By Duke Snider

In 1966, I managed in the Los Angeles Dodgers' minor-league system at Tri-City, Washington, of the Northwest League. Although it wasn't a rookie year, there were many first-year players assembled, both "prospects" and "suspects."

We had a very solid club, led by Roy Gleason, a former bonus-baby outfield prospect from Southern California. Roy played first base and hit .281 with 16 home runs in 74 games with us. Dodger scout Kenny Myers signed Roy out of high school in '61 as a switch-hitter with tremendous power. Two years later, he was pinch-running for the Dodgers during a tight pennant race, and he laced a double in his only at-bat—a perfect 1.000 batting average. But Roy returned to the minors in '64, finding that cracking the Dodgers' all-star outfield, which included two-time batting champion Tommy Davis and world-class sprinter Willie Davis, was harder than he imagined.

While I was still playing with the Dodgers, I had a chance to see Roy in spring training down in Vero Beach, Florida. By the time I saw Roy

Duke Snider. *Courtesy of the Los Angeles Dodgers. All rights reserved.*

again, this time as a manager, I could see that he was the victim of "overcoaching." He was thinking too much at the plate, causing a long, iffy swing. After we switched him to first base, he had a very good season. I got him to forget about thinking at the plate, to just swing hard and drive the ball. Coaches can put too many ideas into a player's head, confusing him, when often those problems solve themselves. Roy ended up enjoying a successful season. Roy and I went our separate ways in 1967, when I was sent to manage AA-Albuquerque and Roy was sent to Vietnam.

Two decades earlier, I'd been drafted into the navy at 18 years old. Towards the end of WWII, I was assigned to a submarine tender that repaired ships when they returned from duty. I wasn't involved in combat, and I was a member of our crew's baseball team, so I played three or four times per week in Guam. For Roy, the situation was much different and far more dangerous.

In this book, you'll discover the range of emotions in his life, from adolescent optimism to the adult understanding of a decorated veteran—one that has a deep appreciation for his country. Today, the United States military faces challenges around the globe, and like Roy, I'm very proud of what those young men and women are trying to accomplish.

Roy's heroism earned him many military citations, including the Purple Heart and the Bronze Star, but the injuries he sustained created a daunting challenge when he attempted to resume his baseball career. As a child in Southern California, Roy grew up with dreams of wearing Dodger blue, and he realized that dream, which is more than many can claim. Most people would give anything for one major-league at-bat. Roy not only got that chance, he succeeded once he got it. Unfortunately, he wasn't granted another chance, and perhaps more unfortunately, that's just part of the game that he so dearly loves.

ACKNOWLEDGMENTS

The authors would like to acknowledge the following people who contributed to and made possible the publishing of this book:

We wish to thank the dynamic publishing team at Sports Publishing L.L.C.—from president Peter Bannon and Mike Pearson, who were the first to recognize the value of this remarkable story, to developmental editor Travis W. Moran, who reduced our many words while preserving the emotional essence of this story. We'd also like to acknowledge Kelley Brown, Randy Fouts, and the promotion and marketing departments, who have helped tell Roy's story to a curious public and remind them that we must never forget our veterans nor our current servicemen and -women.

A very special thank you goes to the Dodgers organization for their recognition of Roy and his accomplishments both on and off the field, and to Duke Snider for writing the foreword. Another big thank you goes to Henry (Hank) Ehrlich, who directed us to those we hope will take this story to the silver screen. In particular, we want to acknowledge those who gave their time through interviews and provided important and valuable information for this book—to the Gleason and Gorr families, residing in California and Illinois; to Roy's sons, Troy and Kaile; to Roy's mother, Molly, to whom this book is dedicated in part and who recently passed away; to Roy's two sisters—Pat (Neiman) and Cathy (Bortz)—their children (Rene, Andy, Neal, David, and Chris), and John. Another thank you goes to Sharron Von Brandis.

Deserved thanks go to the many sportswriters who shared a part of Roy's story with their readers over the years—especially Bill Plaschke from the *Los Angeles Times* and Mike Arkush from *Vietnam Veterans Magazine*.

Also, we'd like to thank all of our friends and associates for providing emotional meat to this book: Mr. and Mrs. Joe Stephenson,

Mike Sgobba, Jim Gilbert, Ron Cey, Paul and Marie Palmquist, Jim Campanis, Bill (Wazy) Wasdyke, Gary Mulleady, John Vanelli, Margie Myers-Escandon, Mickey Hartling, Brent Shyer, Red Adams, Tommy Lasorda, Guy Wellman, Tom Adams, Clarence Jones, Derek Hall, Bob Graziano, Rob Menschel, Ann Marshall—and a very special thank you to Vin Scully and Buzzie Bavasi.

—R.G., W.W., M.L.

Besides all of my family, friends, and those who contributed to this book, I'd like to pay a very special tribute to members of the United States Army, Alpha Company Fighting Falcons 3rd Battalion, 39th Infantry, and 9th Infantry Divisions, with whom I served in Vietnam, including: Rod Gilliland, Paul Davis, Gordan Clapp, Ron (Tanker) Klump, Hershel (Top) Johnson, Lieutenant Madrigal, Dan Gentile, "Mississippi," "Alabama," and Jerry Gapol. I'd also like to acknowledge and salute the following Medal of Honor recipients from the 9th Infantry Division:

Sammy L. Davis	Edward A. Devore
James W. Fous	Don J. Jenkins
Leonard B. Keller	Thomas J. Kinsman
George C. Lang	David P. Nash
Clarence E. Sasser	Mitchell W. Stout
Raymond R. Wright	

Lest we never forget those from the 3rd Battalion, 39th Infantry, and 9th Infantry Divisions who paid the ultimate price with their lives:

PFC Luis G. Mora	PFC Robert F. Vernes
SP4 Gerald F. Novak	SP4 Charles J. Feddema
SP4 Wilbert J. Gresham	SP4 Joseph M. Cagnacci
SP4 Charles R. Moudry	SP4 Robert W. Skarphol
CPL Robert L. Smith	PFC Clarence A. Mooney

SP4 Allen T. Makin, II.
SP4 Thomas D. Darling
PFC Edward J. Haarwaldt
SSG Freddie D. Jones, Sr.
PFC Oscar F. Nicewander
SP4 Robert L. Salinas
SP4 Robert M. Bennett
PFC Bruce G. Ockey
1LT Elwood R. Hendrix
PFC Paul W. Risinger
SGT Patrick J. Long
SP4 Russell K. Blatz
SGT Rainer K. Morgan
CPL Robert E. Young
PFC Alfredo Medina Jr.
2LT John F. Sevick
PFC Charles R. Horton
SP4 Stephen J. Stewart
SGT Franklin A Townsend
PSG Paul E. Jackson
PFC David M. Powell
PFC William J. Matthews
SSG Robert D. Long
SGT Kenneth J. Britt
SP4 Michael A. Blakey
SSG James A. Roberts

2LT Charles W. Brown Jr.
SSG Raymund F. De Herrera
CPT Gary L. Hobbs
PFC Dennis R. Morrell
SP4 James R. Novotny
SP4 Albert Korona III
PFC Jerry L. Holmes
2LT David L. Green, Jr.
CPL Joseph Sosinski
CPL Jimmy L. Fisher
CPL Donald W. Keep
SP4 Robert L. Crawley
SP4 Stephen J. Stewart
SP4 Troy E. Hirni II
CPL James E. Reed
1LT Donald B. Small
PFC Jesse C. Burrough
SSG Jimmy Bedgood
SGT Howard E. Querry
CPL Robert M. Jacobs
SSG Kenneth E. Mattson
PFC Anthony J. Sivo
SP4 James E. Lothman
PFC Lathan Houston
PFC David P. Oker

I would also like to acknowledge my uncle Art for playing catch with me and taking me to the ball games—as well as the entire Gorr family for their great sense of humor. I'd also like to acknowledge the Dennis Hardin family for employing me for many years, and the people I worked for and with at Hardin Honda: Bob and Roberta Bechtloff,

Eric and Kathryn Turner, Terry Hood (who received two Purple Hearts from service in Vietnam), Andy Montoya, Art and Andy Campos, Jim Barton, Thomas Rezepka, Tony Nguyen, Rob Klemenz, Dan Foltz, Freddy Mejia, Dick Baril, Andy Gifford, Renaldo, John Buhs, Scott Bechtloff, Kriste, John Yakel, Jim Marsh, "Coke," John Kiser, Chris Ormsbee, Sherry, Kim, Sandra, Diane, Denise, Lisa, Daryle, Jay Allen, Bill Vazak, Rob, Linda, and Ronnie.

If I didn't remember you here, please know that you're not forgotten.

Thank you.

—R.G.

Before paying tribute to Roy Gleason and Mark Langill, I would like to express my deep appreciation to my wife, Donna, for remaining so supportive during this nearly half decade of work to bring this story to life—and to my daughter, Karie, for her continued faith and dedication along with her business assistance and support; to my son, Bill, and my daughter-in-law, Argelia, and my grandsons Casey, Dillion, Ely, and Finn Wasinack, who love sports and hopefully will continue to play baseball; to my sisters, Joan (Selfridge) and June (Miller), for their never-ending support and love; to Harry Miller, Joe Berlin, and Bob Blumenfeld, who will forever be family heroes to me; to family members, Aldina Fox, Mary Hicks, Dorothy Berlin, Jackie Blumenfeld, Joe Suarez, and the Dusterhoff family (Diane, Jack, Mike, Lori and Terry Lambrecht) and James Berlin for their encouragement and support.

I'd also like to thank my many friends and associates: Ed Engemen; Mike and Dora Poland and family; Don and Tam Issacs; Ray Dewitt; Don and Carol Cotton; Dave and Kathy Porter; Ron Unharriet; Howard Boydstun; Rayleen Thornton; Robert Rosenblatt; Dr. Ethan and Alice Alllen; Brenda and Gary Wiewel and family, Frank Thornton,

Brenda Keiner and family, Charles Lawhon; Jose and Lillia Rodriquez and family; Jan Martin and family; Norma Brunts; Charlie and Mike Doyle; Willie Jacobson; John and Marge Wilson and family; Stuart, (Sr. and Jr.); Tonyea Kane, and Chris Johnson.

A special thank you also goes to Coach John Wooden for his inspiration and class.

To Roy Gleason for allowing me the opportunity to tell his story, and Mark Langill, who truly opened the door—I thank you.

—W.W.

A life filled with blessings also brings gratitude to family, friends, teachers, athletes, and colleagues who made it possible. Special thanks from a proud uncle to Mark and Michael Rayala, the most prolific M-and-M combination since Maris and Mantle—here's hoping you both enjoy blue skies forever.

—M.L.

1
Opening My Eyes

The blinding rays of the midday sun pried open my eyes at a moment when I was unsure where I was and temporarily lost in time. A small cloud moved in front of the sun bringing immediate relief from both overwhelming brightness and searing heat. Lying on my back, I stared into the sun-filled sky, and my mind began to clear. I remembered seeing a flash above me, then feeling the concussion of the blast that knocked me completely off my feet. The muddy irrigation moat where I landed cushioned my fall and probably saved my life.

It was July 24, 1968, and I had been stationed at a remote outpost in South Vietnam for several months. Moments earlier, I'd been walking point as the unit I was leading walked into an ambush that began with the exploding shell above our heads. In a split second, I was flying through the air onto my back. The first thing I recall seeing is the white sun overhead; its brilliant glow eased by a puffy white cloud and the jungle vegetation.

As I lay there that sultry day, my mind raced back to my boyhood home in LaGrange, Illinois—a small town just outside of Chicago where I was born and lived as a young boy. We lived in a rural area—in what was a forest preserve—and I recalled many hot and muggy July afternoons just lying on my back under the trees and looking up at the sun.

LEFT: Roy's father, Richard Roy Gleason, wearing his Seabee uniform during WWII.
From the Roy Gleason Collection

BELOW: Amalia Gorr (Molly) soon to be Mrs. Richard R. Gleason—Roy's mother in her wedding dress, July 11, 1938.
From the Roy Gleason Collection

My earliest recollection of LaGrange was when I was about two and half years old and my dad returned home from World War II. During the war, he served in the Pacific campaign with the Seabees. The Seabees were an armed forces division comprised of engineers and construction personnel assigned to build (or rebuild) our military installations. His primary job included building the landing bases and runways on many of the Pacific islands previously held by the Japanese. Although I was only two and a half, I have a vivid memory of his return home. I remember Mom jumping up from our kitchen table screaming and crying with joy as my dad opened our back door. He held out his big arms as she raced into them. Seconds later, all of us were in his arms and hugging his neck. Even today, I can remember that early moment in my life.

My dad seemed tall and very distinguished in his military uniform. I was born while he was away, during the war, and while Mom had sent him pictures, this was the first time we had seen each other. As he lifted me up in his strong arms, I could see tears rolling down his cheek. Then he asked my mother, "Is this is my son, Roy? Wow, is he big!" For the first time in my life, I now felt our family was complete.

In those early days, our house was filled with joy and laughter. All of us were very happy to be together, yet the mood would change when family and friends would talk about the war. I noticed a sadness that would come over my dad's face and I wondered, "Why?"

When I'd play soldier it was always exciting and fun. It seemed the memories of the war, and the things he saw or went through were things that he didn't enjoy talking about or even recalling. Many years later, I would understand why.

Mom and Dad lived next door to his parents, William (Grandpa Bill), and Grandma Minnie before the war, and when Dad went into the service, Mom stayed. Aunt Marilyn and Uncle Bill also lived next door, so practically all of our neighbors were family. I grew up the middle child, sandwiched between my sister Pat, who is three years older; and my sister Cathy, who is seven years younger. Grandpa (Bill) was the head of the forest preserve, and even though Chicago was not

Grandpa and Grandma Gleason in LaGrange, Illinois, in 1946, where Roy lived until he was 11 years old. *From the Roy Gleason Collection*

far away, we lived in the country. In fact, the only time I saw kids my own age was at the small country school I attended.

Mom's family also lived nearby, in the small town of Maywood. As both families were near one another, we'd spend many weekends visiting, and on holidays, we always got together. Mom came from a large family of 11 children—six sisters and four brothers. I remember two of her brothers vividly: Uncle Fred and Uncle Artie. Both were good athletes and followed sports, causing my mom to say that she thought I got my athletic ability from "her side" of the family.

These comforting family memories started to fade as my eyes focused on the branches that filtered the clouds and the sun. It seemed cool as I lay on my back, but my body was hot and sweating. My mind kept telling me it was one of those sultry Midwestern days, and if you've lived there, you know the type—when it's so hot you sweat just standing still. That's when you pray a breeze will come along. While on my back, shaded from the scorching sun, the cool ground was my only comfort, and it felt good . . . so good. As I closed my eyes, my mind returned home to that young boy who dreamed of playing baseball for the Chicago Cubs, or according to Grandpa Bill, the "Greatest Baseball Team in the World."

As I was growing up in LaGrange, baseball became my life. I remember when I was five or six, with my cowboy outfit on, I'd play soldier and pretend I was with my dad in the war, but when I reached seven, all of that changed. I remember when my Grandpa Bill took me to my first professional game: We sat out in right field at Wrigley Field, and I watched the great Hank Sauer play. From that moment on, baseball was the only activity or sport that captivated my complete interest.

Although Grandpa Bill and Uncles Art and Fred would play catch with me and taught me how to hold the bat, my first real experience of playing baseball came when I was nine years old. That's when I first played baseball with other kids my own age, and I loved it. Because I was big for my age, and could run and throw well, I mainly played shortstop, but my favorite position was pitcher—that's where the action was.

While walking around the forest preserve one day, I started picking out spots on trees to throw little rocks, pretending each was the catcher's glove. I imagined I was pitching in the ninth inning of the World Series and just threw the game-winning pitch to end the game. I could hear the crowd cheering, and as I looked into the stands, my entire family was cheering for me. I became really good at throwing rocks and at hitting where I aimed. Then something happened I truly regretted. I saw a rabbit and thought I'd scare it, but instead, the rock I threw found its mark, and the innocent animal died that day. I remember crying as I buried it. I didn't want to kill it or want it to die, but it did. I'll never forget that tragic day and the deep sadness I felt, being responsible for ending its life. From that day on, I never threw another rock at any other innocent animals.

≈ ≈ ≈

Though mere seconds passed, time had been suspended, but my mind started to clear. Suddenly, I began to imagine flies, mosquitoes, and warrior fire ants were about to attack me. That thought helped reality return. I realized I wasn't in LaGrange—while we had flies, mosquitoes, and ants in LaGrange, they were not like these.

The ants in Vietnam are called "red warrior" ants, and they travel along the branches and vines in the jungle. The unique thing about these ants is that once they get on to your body or clothing they work up your body to your neck and face and then bite or sting the hell out of you. These were ants straight from hell.

The mosquitoes were equally as vicious as the warrior ants, and they were everywhere. They not only attack in mass or swarm, but they suck your blood, and it felt like they were eating you alive. They spread fatal diseases like malaria that required taking tablets to prevent infection. Although the tablets often gave us diarrhea, that side affect, while unpleasant, was far better than the alternative. There were some of our guys that, for whatever reason, didn't take the tablets, and a number paid the price in extreme illness or death.

As I became more aware of my surroundings, I was no longer that little boy dreaming of playing baseball and living in a wonderful small town in America. I heard yelling, screaming, and I realized that one of my platoon members was lying motionless face up nearby; he'd suffered extensive wounds and appeared lifeless. His name was Anthony (Tony) Sivo; he was my machine gunner and only 19 years old. I called his name but received no reply.

The explosion that had knocked me off my feet had also released shrapnel that had ended Tony's life instantly. When you're on the front lines, you learn and understand that you could check out instantly, but that didn't make looking at his lifeless body any easier. Moments before, he was a young, healthy, and vibrant young American whose life was taken in an instant in a land half a world away from home. He, like all of us, believed we were on a mission fighting for freedom and democracy. We were there to save a weak country from a ruthless communist government. We also were there to protect America from the "Domino Effect." After all, that's what President Johnson, his advisors, and the generals were saying.

"If Vietnam falls to the communists, that could lead to the rest of Asia, like dominoes, and ultimately lead to the entire world."

We had to stem the tide here—rather than on the beaches and shores of America. [1]

During my life, I've learned that world events set in motion years before one is even born may come to touch our lives many years or decades later, and those same events may affect you directly and choose your path for you. When President Eisenhower made this statement and our government instituted our "Indochina Policy," I was nine years old. Sixteen years later, that policy had brought me to a place where I didn't want to be and put my life and the lives of thousands of other Americans in grave jeopardy.

Although I was 25 then, I frankly hadn't paid much attention to what was happening in the world. Perhaps, like most people, I was caught up in my own world, trying to accomplish my dream. I recall newspaper and television reports of the 1960 presidential campaign between John F. Kennedy and Richard Nixon and their famous "debates." [2]

After President Kennedy's assassination, news reports indicated that President Johnson agreed with his military advisors that we needed to stop the communists in Vietnam the way we had in Korea. He sent more military personnel to protect our military advisors (MAs) who were being kidnapped or killed by the Viet Cong (VC). As a result, we became more involved than ever. As history shows, it wasn't too long before we sent more troops and took over the majority of the fighting. Unlike in Korea, we did not have total UN support, and a significant percentage of South Vietnamese were also fighting against us and thought of us as aliens and the real enemy.

Even today, I question whether Tony had to die at all, or whether any of my original Ninth Infantry Company should have died or been wounded. That's what still haunts me at night, particularly when I hear a chopper overhead. Now if one flies over the house at night, I'll hear it and wake up wondering where I am and if I'm still in that battle for my life.

Our casualty counts were high, even though the enemy losses were far greater than ours were. Our feeling was that if we lost one man, it was one too many. Of our original company of 90 infantrymen who arrived with me, I believe, only one member, Steve Mallory, managed to get through alive and unwounded. To my knowledge, Steve was the only one who made it, but since being wounded, I have not had any contact with him since the war. The fact remains that half of our company was wounded or badly maimed, and the other half died there and paid the ultimate price—leaving unfinished lives and families to grieve forever.

The seconds that followed the explosion on that fateful day were filled with the sounds of grenades and artillery explosions, M-16s and AK-47s. Machine gun fire was going on all around, and I began to realize this nightmare was real. I could hear yelling and shouting, and it was apparent some of our men had been hit. In the flash of that explosion, many memories swirled through my mind and touched my dreams. Now the dream had disappeared, and a nightmare took its place. The experience was so dark and painful that, the only way I can describe it is that I felt as if the curtain of ultimate evil was enveloping us all.

I knew I had to return fire as quickly as possible or run the risk of having the enemy rush my position and possibly be shot at point blank range. I felt something warm and wet on my arm.

Seeing the blood from my wounded wrist, I quickly made a tourniquet to stop the blood flow. At first, I didn't feel the shrapnel in my lower leg. The adrenaline pumping through my body and the instinct to survive helped overcome the pain.

I was point man for my infantry unit. As point man, you're the person out front. Your job is to lead your squad, spot any potential dangers, and advise the commanding officer (CO) if a different path or direction should be taken. We'd been on patrol for many months, and prior to our ambush, I'd advised our CO of just such a danger. I kept reliving the moments that led us into this ambush. Just minutes before, I told our CO, who'd only joined our unit a few days earlier, that his orders were "putting us in real danger of ambush and booby traps."

The asshole said, "Sgt. Gleason, I am in command," and insisted we follow his orders, taking us down the well-traveled path.

He didn't die that day, nor was he wounded. I don't know where the son of a bitch is today, but if he's still around—and if he has a conscience—he's carrying the loss of Tony Sivo and three other brave men who died in that split second under his command. That foolish decision includes all of us who were wounded that day as well. Wherever he is, he'll have to carry that day and what happened to us for the rest of his damn life and if he believes in one, even into the hereafter.

As I rolled on my belly to return fire, I didn't have time to think about the reason I was there. Why am I fighting to the death—an enemy I didn't even know—in a world far removed from the small mid-American town of LaGrange, Illinois? The sight of blood-soaked mud was now the scene, and God . . . how I missed the lush green baseball fields I'd played on in America. I didn't have time to think about what I did nor whom I might have offended in my twenty-five plus years to end up in this God-forsaken place. Even though I was one of the oldest in my unit, I believed I had more time ahead of me and a hell of a lot more to do with my life. I certainly did not want it to end here, in this muddy, blood-soaked moat. I believe all of us who were there that day were thinking the same thing.

That firefight may go on forever in my mind, but finally it ended. There was silence, and it seemed to last an eternity. Finally, I—along with the other wounded and the buddies who didn't make it (the official term is "killed in action" or KIA)—was evacuated by helicopter.

As I slipped in and out of consciousness, I thought about Tony Sivo and the others, and what we'd talked about during that morning, the last we'd ever spend together—things like what our dreams were, what we missed most about home, and what we planned to do when we got back.

Tony said he had a girlfriend back home, and when he got out, he hoped they'd get married and raise a family. He also told me that, wherever he was, he'd follow my baseball career. He said, "Roy, when you're playing in the majors with the Dodgers, even though I'm not a big Dodger fan, I'll still root for you. And when you are playing nearby, I'll be there, sitting right in the stands, and I'll introduce you to my beautiful wife."

I said that'd be great, and when he came to the game—no matter whether we won or lost—I'd take him and his wife out to dinner, and we'd celebrate. I reminded him that we first both had to get out of this place alive and in one piece. I'll never forget Tony or the brief and special time we shared.

Looking back on that day, I regret there wasn't something more I could've done to save his life. Why didn't I see the M-155 hidden in the trees above our heads? I learned after being hit, that it was command-detonated as we walked underneath it. Why hadn't the new CO listened to me about traveling down "well-beaten paths"?

Those with battle experience in Vietnam knew you never followed a "well-traveled or beaten path," and only rarely did you take the same route twice. Our objective was to keep the VC guessing, and by not following the same paths, you were less likely to be ambushed. However, on this particular day, our new CO insisted we stay on the same "well-beaten" path, and as a result, we walked right into the ambush. I thought if only I would have insisted or refused the direct order, Sivo might be alive today. Sure the CO could have had me court-martialed or could have even shot me, but at least we wouldn't have lost those men that day. Even as I think about it 40 years later, I still have a tough time accepting what happened on July 24, 1968, and the brave friends who were lost.

The sound of the chopper's propellers and its vibration tended to dull my senses. Whether I was going into shock or half-consciousness, my mind continued to wander. Perhaps to keep from losing it and to try to escape the insanity I'd been through, my thoughts turned to the past—to the carefree days in the summer sun with my parents, my sister Pat, and baby sister Cathy; and the times we shared with our grandparents, aunts, and uncles in LaGrange. I didn't realize it at the time, but life simply doesn't get any better. . . .

⟡ ⟡ ⟡

I was what they call a "war baby," and born on April 9, 1943, to Molly and Richard Gleason. At the time of my birth, my dad and our nation were in the middle of World War II. He was serving with the Seabees in the Pacific campaign, fighting the Japanese.

Two months before I was born, our troops defeated the Japanese in the battle at Guadalcanal in some of the costliest and bloodiest fighting of the war. The news of that conflict and the high losses we sustained in the battles with the Japanese were worrisome to my parents' families.

During that time, the most famous war correspondent was Ernie Pyle. The newspapers were filled with his eyewitness accounts of the battles and bravery of our men. He covered it all, from North Africa to Europe to the Pacific campaign. Sadly, he died on April 18, 1945, in the middle of one of the war's bloodiest battles. The reports said he was killed as he and other American GIs were shot by a machine gunner during the battle of Iwo Jima. Many journalists say that Ernie Pyle was the "eyes and ears" of the American GI. He preferred to be on the front lines, "where the action was." He wanted the folks at home to know the "frontline story"—that war is not glamorous, and courage under the siege of battle was the true test of human character and that of which real heroes are made. Ernie Pyle was a true hero and paid the ultimate price with his own life.

In April of 1943, the most important story of the time was the war, and it affected everyone's life in one way or another. The week I was born, President Roosevelt, as part of an executive order, froze all prices and wages. That stopped various companies from taking advantage of shortages and other situations the war had created. At the same time, the government released the somber statistics that over 60,000 Americans had died in the war to that point.

As a child of that war, I was insulated totally from all the sad news. Neither Mom nor Dad's family ever allowed me to know that they were worried about my father, even though they must have been. At that point in time, while most of the world was in chaos, I was growing up in the peace and tranquillity of a beautiful forest preserve in Middle America, far away from that terrible war.

I spent over 10 formative years growing up in LaGrange. I was, and always have been, closest to my mom, and I presume that's because I didn't see my dad nearly as much. I'm sure it was because he was in the service and away during the war. Even after the war, he spent a great deal of time away from home. He bought an 18-wheel truck and that took him away for long periods. So, for the first 10 years of my life, I just didn't get the time or the chance to really know my dad.

However, there was one very "special time" that my dad and I shared that I will never forget. I had just turned 10, school had ended, and summer vacation was just beginning.

"Roy," Dad said. "You're growing up so fast, how would you like to go with me on my next cross-country trip in the truck?" He didn't have to ask me twice; I immediately responded by asking, "You mean it? Can I really go with you? What if Mom says no?"

He said he would talk to Mom about it.

I was impressed and surprised that he didn't ask my sister Pat, who was older—not that I think she'd have had any interest in going, even though she was a typical tomboy. But he asked me, and it represented the first time the two of us would be alone together for a fairly long duration, and I was excited about that. I could tell my mom was not as keen on this idea as my dad, but he assured her that it would be good for me; and besides, she wouldn't have to put up with me for a couple of weeks. Dad had a convincing way about him, and when Mom said okay, I thought everything was right in the world.

Although I loved playing baseball, Dad was not really into sports much. He didn't seem to be particularly interested in most professional sports and definitely didn't share Grandpa Bill's love and enthusiasm for the "Greatest Baseball Team in the World"—the Chicago Cubs. I didn't see my dad as often as most kids, and we didn't share many of the same interests. But that only fueled my desire to make my father proud of me. His invitation to join him on this trip was just the chance I needed.

The trip we took that summer turned out to be a cross-country journey, starting in Chicago and ending in Los Angeles, California. It was about 5,000 miles round-trip. During this time together, I discovered that Dad had a great sense of humor, telling me jokes and funny stories along the way. I think he was both happy and proud to have his son riding along with him; and while he didn't say at the time, he probably hoped I would follow in his footsteps.

Although Mom was the main disciplinarian in the family, I knew that if she couldn't handle the problem, my dad would. When we were at home or visiting friends, he could be strict and hand out the punishment if necessary; fortunately, that rarely occurred. All it would take was for Mom to say, "Richard, the kids (generally Roy) are not behaving," and he'd give us (or me) that "ice cold" look. I knew I had gone as far as I could go before pain and disaster surely would follow. While I was at his side on that trip, I discovered he was really a kind, gentle man—so much more than the perceived father who was rarely around and would not tolerate bad behavior.

I'll never forget the thrill when Dad asked, while we were driving along a straight, endless stretch of highway, if I would like to drive for a while. He knew that even though I was only 10, I had driven before. In fact, Grandpa Bill would let me drive his tractor in the fields near the forest preserve, and Dad had even let me drive the car around the driveway at home.

"Roy," he said. "All I want you to do is to steer straight ahead while I take a little cat nap."

Although I said, "Sure," I have to admit I was damn scared. What if something ran out in front of us? Or God forbid, if I had to slam on the brakes? Although I was nervous when he had me slide over him and grab that big wheel, I told him that I'd be fine, and he didn't have to worry. Who was I kidding? Now I was driving a 18-wheeler, filled with valuable cargo, down a state highway. Although I was big for my age, I could barely see over the dashboard and had to look between the space on the steering wheel. Just before he drifted into sleep, he said, "When you see a car or if you have any trouble just blow the horn" to wake him up. At 10 years old, that request seemed appropriate and logical, after all, my dad wouldn't put me, himself, the truck, and cargo in any real danger. Besides, I knew he was tired, and that highway ahead was as straight as a string, everything would be fine.

Just steer . . .

Well as fate would have it, nothing impeded our progress. As I drove down that highway, gripped that big truck wheel, and felt the hum of the engine and all 18 wheels on the highway, I became more and more confident. As the first car met me on the highway, I glanced over at Dad, who was sound asleep, and just kept on trucking.

"Don't blow the horn," I thought. "Let him sleep, you're doing just fine."

A few miles down the two-lane highway, I passed several cars that seemed to be going at a snail's pace. As we passed by, I could see the people in the car look over and see this 10-year-old kid driving this big truck. You should have seen the double takes; I smiled about it then and still laugh about it today. They probably were wondering who was driving this big truck since my head was just barely above the steering wheel. I wouldn't condemn my dad for doing this, nor would I allow my kids at that age to do what he allowed me to do. In reflection, it wasn't smart, because accidents do happen. I also know there are many ways that society sets up so-called standards for becoming a man. I believe on that hot summer day, along that long, straight highway going to California, that event made me feel like a man for the first time.

When Dad finally woke up, he asked, "How long have I been asleep?"

"About an hour," I replied.

At first, he couldn't believe it, but then he looked at his watch, and said, "Why in the hell didn't you wake me up sooner? Why didn't you honk the horn? Did you see or pass any cars?"

"I did see a few cars," I told him. "But I didn't want to wake you up."

At first, he was upset. . . . No, that's not quite right, he was real upset. . . . No, that's not quite right, he was mad! Damn mad! He began, as Mom would say, "using the Lord's name in vain," followed by a few other profanities and finished by telling me how wrong I was and describing the dangers of what could have happened. After what seemed like an endless tirade, he started to calm down. Later, he even started to laugh a little when he thought about the people's faces as his 10-year-old son passed them.

That trip and that day were very special for a couple of personal reasons. One, it showed my dad had both faith and confidence that I could do a man's job. Secondly, I performed the job, and I will forever thank God that no one was hurt. He did mention, as we were approaching home, that he "would prefer that we keep my truck-driving experience between the two of us. . . . " and so it remains to this day.

One more thing I learned on that special trip with my dad was that he liked California. He liked the warm climate, but even in 1953, he thought it was too crowded and had too much traffic. When Dad mentioned to Mom that he liked California, my mom was ecstatic; he had an aunt and uncle living in Southern California and thought it might be good to move there. Mom was tired of the long, cold winters and the hot, humid summers in LaGrange. I think she also felt isolated living at the forest preserve, she saw California as the *ideal* place to live because of the weather and all the things you could see and do there. She'd tell my dad that California was the perfect place to raise a family,

This house in LaGrange, Illinois, served as Roy's home until he was 11 years old.
From the Roy Gleason Collection

because there was affordable new housing, good schools, and more job opportunities.

Mom and Dad had many discussions about moving to California in 1953, and they would even ask Pat and I what we thought about a transition. Moving didn't excite me. LaGrange was my home, the only home I had ever known, and while I enjoyed traveling and saw California with my dad, I never really thought about moving there. After many discussions, the decision was finally made, and in the summer of 1954, Dad and Mom announced to my sisters and me that we were moving to Southern California.

At first, I took this decision as quite earth-shattering, because while my parents had talked many times about moving, I never thought we would. After all, LaGrange was our home, we would be leaving my grandparents, my aunts and uncles, and this wonderful and beautiful place. We'd be moving to who knows where, living in a new area where we didn't know anyone. Chances are, we would have to live in "the City" instead of the country, and I wouldn't have my own baseball field.

Because I was somewhat shy and sheltered, I'd have to make new friends for the first time and go to what, to me, would be a crowded school. This was something I was not eagerly anticipating. Later, I discovered that moving to California wasn't really what all of us wanted. We also learned we had company—millions of Midwesterners and everyone else were moving to Southern California.

Leaving our home in LaGrange wasn't easy. It was particularly sad for me to leave my grandfather and uncles because they had always encouraged me about playing baseball. The saddest moment was leaving "my ball field." I designed it myself, and it was in the back of our house. I had gotten into a ton of trouble when I chopped down a cherry tree that was right in the middle of the field and in the way of everything. I was in trouble for two big reasons. Mom loved cherries, and this was her favorite tree; and being on a forest preserve, you are not allowed to chop down trees, ball field or not.

Before leaving for California, I went out and said goodbye to my ball field, the place where I would play catch with my grandpa and uncles. This was my special place, where I imagined hitting World Series-winning home runs and pitching no-hitters against the greatest players of all time. That "special place" was my "Field of Dreams," so as I said goodbye for the very last time, I buried something very special under home plate. Time and progress have erased the field and what I buried there that day.

≈ ≈ ≈

Again, the vibration of the chopper engines dulled my senses, but as we flew over bush and rice paddies toward base camp, the adrenaline that had dulled my pain was ebbing. I knew the wounds to my wrist and the shrapnel in my calf were not life-threatening, but I prayed they would not end my baseball career.

I learned some time later from my sisters that, on the same day I was wounded, my mother awoke from a sound sleep half a world away to tell them ". . . something serious has happened to Roy." A few days later, her premonition was confirmed.

As we continued to base camp, my mind recalled the events that had taken place just hours earlier. I could still see the smiling faces of Tony Sivo and the other men in our platoon. I remembered the discussion of the hellish schedule we were under the night before and for the last several months.

Our standing orders included both day (search and destroy) and night (ambush patrol) missions. We were air-lifted into areas for search and destroy missions, and these were specifically designed for us to "make contact" with the enemy. Our night-ambush patrols were always on foot, designed to surprise the enemy. Our orders were "not to fire unless fired upon." Because of the many casualties we were suffering, our personnel constantly kept changing. In short, this meant because of the continuous loss of men, new recruits were taking their places. In some respects, this situation kept us from getting very close to one another. It's never easy to see one of your own men hit, but seeing a friend wounded or killed is far worse. At the same time, when you're in a battle, it's critical to know the people who are fighting with you, to know their capabilities and whether you can count on them or not. The newer the recruit, the less you knew about his abilities in a firefight.

One positive that the COs kept preaching was that "Charlie" (VC) was taking casualties that were 90 to 95 percent higher than ours. That might've helped keep the morale up for the troops, but tell that to the grieving wife and the fatherless child—to them, it was really meaningless.

In addition to Tony Sivo, our assistant machine gunner and another platoon member lost their lives later in the hospital. Just two months earlier, Clyde Guerra—a great young guy who was in our unit—was hit and died in the hospital a week later. I was just getting to know him when it happened. It was tough to take.

All of these men were some of the bravest and best fighting men this nation has ever known, and even after many years, I still remember their faces and feel their absence.

Tony was only 19 years old when his life was taken. He stood about six foot three with a solid build. He had a good head of hair, and his brown eyes would light up when he'd joke about the war and when he'd talk about his girl and going home. He'd been with me on patrols before, and I knew I could count on him when I was walking point for back up and support.

Unfortunately, I didn't get to know many of the other men as well as Tony, and I don't remember where they called home. I do recall them asking me about playing baseball in the major leagues. They couldn't believe I was on the front lines with them.

They all would say, "Sarge, what in the hell did you do to be sent here?"

I'd laugh and say, "I still don't know, but what in the hell did all of you do to be here with me?"

We'd laugh and then go about our business. But this day would be the last time that I'd see them alive. I regret I didn't get to know them better.

Gordan Clapp was another in our company I remember well. He was hit about a week before I was, and I didn't see him until we were both in the hospital. The wounds he received were far more serious than mine were. Gordan's a great guy, and I told him he should go into the movies because he reminded me of Clark Gable—with a pencil-thin mustache. He is a real class act. I was very happy to hear from him recently and learn that he recovered, and we're looking forward to getting together again.

Another friend, Marcellus Lee, was killed in action during his first week in Vietnam. I had the pleasure of meeting him when we were sent to Fort Polk, in Louisiana for additional training. Marcellus was huge; he stood six foot seven and was solid muscle.

On one particular weekend at Fort Polk, a few of the non-commission officers (non-coms) decided to hold some amateur boxing matches, and Marcellus signed up. He had several matches, and although he was not an experienced boxer, his size and strength prevailed, and he literally destroyed everyone he faced.

I was sitting in the audience enjoying each of the matches and cheering Marcellus on when several of my so-called buddies began chanting my name to entice me into the squared circle. At first, I said no way, but after some continuous taunting, I reluctantly climbed into the ring. Although I was in great shape, I told Marcellus, "Hey, I'm no boxer, so let's just put on a show for the guys and dance around."

He assured me he would go easy on me, and that made me feel somewhat at ease. Well, as we danced around the ring just sparring, I think Marcellus was getting tired, so he hit me a real good one. As a result, we really got into it, and so did the crowd. After a number of rounds, they finally called it, when he said it was enough. I don't know if he was really tired due to his earlier bouts or the fact that he didn't want to hurt me; but whatever it was, I was glad it was over. I still remember that a couple of days following the match, we got together and had a few beers and some laughs—that turned out to be the last time I saw him.

Because I went for additional training, he was shipped to Vietnam several weeks before me. I will never forget him or the deep, sinking feeling I had when I heard he was killed during his first week in Vietnam.

᷍ ᷍ ᷍

On the chopper, my mind was still spinning and in an instant raced back to how the day began. We had left base camp at 0600 hours and flew inland with orders to "make contact with the enemy." We had been performing a night patrol in a different area about five hours earlier. We were now used to getting just a few hours of sleep, and we were entering the monsoon season, making our missions hot, humid, and much more difficult and dangerous.

Each day we went to different areas to "make contact" and take or secure the area. Then a week or two later, we would go out and take the same damn area all over again. To most of us, this seemed like a ridiculous way to fight and win a war. As we flew over the Vietnam landscape, no one said much, and we all knew we were going back into hell and harm's way.

As we touched down (we would literally hit the ground running because the chopper was an easy target), we were off in seconds and fanned out through the rice paddy. At approximately 0700, the sky was blue but cloudy, and it was already starting to get hot as we proceeded into the jungle. Our new CO, who had only been in command a few days and had little or no battle experience, now led us. Most of us in the unit thought he was out of West Point or some state side reserve unit, and we were all concerned.

Our infantry unit had taken a very high percentage of casualities, particularly among our officers. In fact, four were killed, and one was severely wounded a few months earlier in one single mortar blast at what we called "The French Fort," and later we called it "Fort Courage." The wounded officer received extensive damage to his leg, and eventually the leg had to be amputated.

Because of the high number of losses among our officers, we were being supplied with COs who were not battle tested and not truly ready for what they had to do. In life, there's is a big difference between the theoretical or ideal situations in which you learn to perform growing up and the truth we call "reality." Nevertheless, our new CO was in command, and his orders were to "make contact with the enemy" in the area we were now going through.

As mentioned earlier, you never take the same path twice in war. The reasoning is simple: if the enemy knows that you continually use one route, ambushing you is much easier to orchestrate.

As we left the rice paddy and moved into the jungle, we could see signs that the enemy was there, and it would only be a matter of time until we made contact. We had done this type of mission before, both night and day. Most of us preferred the day—simply because we had better vision. This was before the modern night-vision goggles were readily available.

Since I had more battle experience than most of our company, I was the point man—as point man, it's not only your own life that concerns you, but also the lives of each of the men following you. I thought at the time that I was good at my job, and I still believe I was, but I'll admit that on that July 24, 1968, I needed to be better.

As time passed, we moved into heavier jungle, and we were nearing a stream. The monsoons that brought heavy and continuous rain over many days had begun, causing the stream to move swiftly but less than waist deep. We began following a well-traveled path that ran along the side of the stream. As point man, I motioned to the CO that we should cross the stream rather than continue along the path. He overruled my suggestion and ordered us to continue down the path.

That decision and order cost the lives of three of my men, not including the two other men who were wounded. Since all three were killed by the M-155 hanging in the trees above us—command detonated by "Charlie"—had we simply crossed the stream, we could have surprised the enemy and most likely prevented casualties. The CO's decision to "follow that well-traveled path" will forever burn in my memory because he may have thought it was easier or quicker than crossing the stream. I've learned in my life that in most cases, experience is really the best teacher. In my mind, the CO failed all of my men and me that day.

Regarding that M-155 that exploded, the weapon was actually one of our own shells that apparently did not detonate upon impact. The VC weren't dumb, they'd pick up our unexploded shells and set them in trees with a charge, waiting until we were triangulated to detonate them. Obviously, the enemy viewed this with great satisfaction, as ironically, they were using our own weapons to kill and wound our men.

When the M-155 went off, the sudden flash knocked me completely off my feet—the sudden pain, the sight and loss of my men—to this day, that single event still gives me nightmares, and I will probably take them to my grave.

In some sense, although I never asked, perhaps the same types of images invaded my dad's dreams and the memories of what he had to encounter when he was in World War II. I imagine anyone who's been in intense combat will understand that sometimes you may even want to fight off sleep. I'm not surprised that many veterans—particularly those who've stared death in the face and seen the destruction in battle—do not want to talk about it. If they're like I am, they want to forget all about that terrible experience. Frankly, the hardest part of telling my story is recalling my Vietnam experiences.

Who wants to remember or recall a nightmare of hell?

I don't know how long it took to be evacuated after I was wounded, and I refused help until all my men had been treated. I do remember a big guy appeared out of nowhere, just after the firing stopped. He picked me up like a sack of potatoes (I'm not small, I'm six foot five and weighed over 200 pounds); slung me over his shoulder, and got me on that chopper in what seemed like seconds. To this day, I don't know who he was, but I owe him my life, and I'll never forget his act of bravery.

As I lay in the belly of the chopper, I tried to erase the scene of what had just transpired. I consider myself to be strong in adversity, and I was taught not to be too emotional; but as I saw the faces of my men behind body-bag zippers, I felt tears running down my cheeks. I remembered them—men who only moments earlier were full of life, hopes, and dreams, and now their lives were gone.

My feelings at that time were filled with three major emotions. One was deep sadness for their loss. The second was hate and vengeance—not only for the enemy who took their lives, but for our CO who had neglected my advice. The third was guilt, brought upon by his orders.

The injection I received on the chopper seemed to dull my emotional state and eased the pain. The roar of the chopper blades seemed louder than usual as we lifted off the battlefield and headed for the base-camp hospital and safety. I again faded in and out of consciousness. My mind and thoughts returned to the little town of LaGrange, Illinois—to a simpler time, when my life seemed whole and safe.

≈ ≈ ≈

I n seconds, I could see that young boy lying on his back with his eyes gazing at the blue Midwestern sky, protected from the noonday sun by the shade of pine and amber trees. It was as though I was looking down from heaven at my young boyhood life on that beautiful forest preserve. There it was! I could see my ball field, and as I floated above, I noticed my mom was walking out to the back yard, hanging the wash on the line. There, in the shade of some fruit trees, was my dad and Grandpa, probably talking about the weather or California.

It was the time in my youth when there was only family and no real talk of war. It was during the early 1950s, and although Dad and grandpa would talk about a strange place called Korea—where Americans were fighting and dying—I felt safe because all my family were here at home together.

During that period, one of my all-time favorite baseball players, Ted Williams, crash-landed his jet aircraft safely after flying a combat mission in Korea. I had his baseball card, and was happy to hear he was okay and would be returning to play baseball for the Boston Red Sox.

In January of 1953, before turning 10 years old, my family and I watched President "Ike" Eisenhower being sworn into office on our small screen television. At the time, I didn't think much about this, but I had listened to my parents say that, before becoming president, he was our top general in World War II. I thought that since everyone was at home and my dad was not away at war, he must have been doing a good job, so in 1953, when he was elected president, I thought it was good news.

Outside of my California trip, the thing I remember most about 1953 was watching the exciting World Series between the New York

Roy's Grandpa Gleason steps to the plate in LaGrange, Illinois.
From the Roy Gleason Collection

Yankees (The Bronx Bombers) and the Brooklyn Dodgers (The Bums) on television with my grandpa and uncle. The series was exciting, and while I was not a Dodger fan, I preferred them to the Yankees. The Yankees won it in six games. Grandpa Bill said the Yankees always won. Most of the time, they did.

Like most kids my age, I collected baseball cards that came in packages of gum. The gum was okay, but the real value was the baseball cards. The World Series seemed even more interesting because many of the top players from both teams were among the cards I had in my collection. I would look at them and dream that, one day, I'd be one of those players with my own baseball card, playing for the Chicago Cubs—The "Greatest Baseball Team in the World"—and we'd beat those darn Yankees.

I could just see it: I am on the mound in Yankee Stadium pitching for the Chicago Cubs against the Yankees. It's now the bottom of the ninth inning, in the seventh and deciding game of the World Series, and I'm facing one of the greatest hitters in baseball, Mickey Mantle. In just his third year in the major leagues, he hit close to .300 and many said he would be the best baseball player in the world. He also is credited with hitting the longest home run in baseball history—565 feet—that same year. When I faced him, though, that didn't scare me—even though the bases were loaded with two outs, and we had a one-run lead. I knew I only had one job to do, and that was to get him out; not let them score the tying or winning runs.

I got into this situation because I was chosen to relieve the starting pitcher in the bottom of the ninth inning. Phil Cavarretta, the Cubs' manager, said, "Roy, it's up to you to win or lose this series. I know you can do it, and so does your grandpa."

The inning began when I got Jerry Collins, the Yankee lead-off first baseman, to hit a fly ball to center field for the first out. Then Billy Martin, the Yanks' second baseman, hit a line drive right up the middle and over my head for a base hit. With one on and one out, I faced the ever-dangerous Phil Rizzuto, the Yankee shortstop, and he managed to work me to a full count and then I lost him on a walk. Now with two on and the lead runner in scoring position, I knew I had to reach for more as Gil McDougald came to the plate. With two balls and two strikes, I got him to go for a high fast ball and struck him out. We now had two outs with two men on base.

The next person to bat was Yogi Berra. To me, he was the most famous catcher in baseball and someone I both feared and admired. He had won many games with his clutch hitting, and I felt he was the most dangerous of all the Yankees at that time. Although I was noted for having pinpoint control and rarely walked many batters, I believe I pitched Yogi too carefully and ended up walking him. Now I was really upset with myself, because I had now put both the tying and winning runs in scoring position due to walks. I could see the nervousness on Phil's face as he paced back and forth in the dugout. The crowd at Yankee Stadium was on its feet, making more noise than I had ever heard before, and I searched the crowd to see Grandpa Bill. I knew both of us were saying our prayers as the public address announcer announced the next batter: "Mickey Mantle." The crowd went wild.

I watched as Mickey came to the plate. His body language was full of confidence, and all the pressure of the seventh and deciding game (and the entire season) was now on the line. He was a switch hitter, and since I was the best right-handed pitcher on the Cubs, he decided to bat left-handed against me.

On my first pitch, I reached back with all my strength and threw it as hard and as fast as I could, but the ball sailed high and was called a ball. The second pitch was another smoking fast ball at the knees that he took for a strike. With that, the fans in Yankee Stadium began to quiet, and the tension began to build.

With a one-and-one count, I decided to throw him a changeup, and I was both relieved and excited when he took a powerful swing and missed it completely. With one ball and two strikes, I reached back and threw another fast ball. It tailed off the corner for another ball. Now you could really feel the tension—the count was now even: two and two. I summoned all the strength and courage I had. After shaking off the catcher, I decided to throw my changeup, but this time Mickey was waiting for it. An unbelievable roar erupted as the fans stood to follow a long, hard line drive head into the upper deck in right field; but I was saved when the ball curved and ended up being a 370-foot foul ball.

So with the count even and the fans cheering their loudest, I reached back and threw another fast ball and again it sailed upward, out of the strike zone. With a full count and no way out, I knew there was no more tomorrow.

Everything came down to one pitch. I thought about my grandpa cheering me on in the stands. I knew that, no matter what happened, he would still love me, but I remembered all those sunny days when we'd play catch, and he'd tell me ". . . Someday, you're going to be a great baseball player." I just couldn't let him down. My parents and sisters were there, as were my aunts and uncles, I could not let any of them down. So with all the strength and courage I could muster, I threw the ball as hard as I could. I watched Mickey's eyes widen as he swung at the perfect pitch with fifty thousand fans in the stands jumping to their feet, and I felt this tremendous jarring that made it seem like the entire stadium was moving.

$$\approx \quad \approx \quad \approx$$

I t was our chopper—it had just hit some air turbulence and reality returned.

It was a dream, but it seemed so real. I didn't want it to end because I had to know if Mickey hit the ball or struck out. If he hit the ball, did he get a base hit, or did he hit it right to someone for the third out? I wanted to know. Then suddenly we were touching down and with that came a flurry of activity.

As we landed at base camp, my mind snapped back to what I'd been through, the men we lost, the others who were wounded, and those still out there on patrol and on the front lines. I was placed on the gurney quickly, wondering what my future would hold in the days, months, and years to follow.

I hadn't had such an unsure feeling about my future since leaving my boyhood home in LaGrange and my trauma as it was confirmed that my parents had finally decided to move to California.

That was in 1954.

Prior to hearing the news that we would be moving, one big news story in '54 involved another baseball hero of mine, Joe DiMaggio, when he married Marilyn Monroe. I was 11 at the time, and girls didn't yet interest me.

"Roy, remember, there are many benefits to being a baseball hero," Grandpa would say with a smile. "First, most people have to work and work hard their entire lives. If you're a great baseball player, you get paid very well for playing a game, and that's not work. Second, you get to meet many beautiful ladies, and if you're as good as 'Joltin' Joe,' you could end up marrying a movie star. Would you like to go out and play catch?"

Years later, I remembered what he said, and it was true.

It was also in 1954 that I received my first polio shot. It was the Salk polio vaccine and was a medical breakthrough, literally stamping out a dreaded disease that often infected children. For years, the newspapers were filled with stories about the many children afflicted by polio. Mom worried that her three kids could possibly get this disease, and she thought it was a medical miracle that a cure had been discovered.

Why did I remember 1954? Was it because of the deep feeling of sadness and insecurity of being uprooted suddenly from my boyhood home in LaGrange? Or was it leaving the only place that I'd ever really known? The flashback ended with the sun rising as we left our home for California. I wondered how we could leave half of our family—my grandparents, aunts, and uncles—behind?

The constant flashbacks in time may have been my mind's way of dealing with the horror and brutality of war. In an instant, Tony had died, two others were near death, and for whatever reason, I had survived. The flashbacks took me away from the pain of the physical and emotional wounds I received.

I've heard it said that, in near-death experiences, your life flashes by in an instant. Mine certainly did. I remember being carried off the chopper, and my last flashback was leaving our home in LaGrange and moving to California.

Fourteen years later, I was lying on a gurney staring up into a blinding sun, bleeding and wounded in a war-torn land half the globe away from home. I was worried about what the future held for me. Was the worst over? Would I have a chance to play baseball again; or did my dream of returning to the major leagues die in that blood-soaked mud on that Vietnam battlefield?

[1] *In April 1954, President Eisenhower introduced the "Domino Theory." At a press conference, he said that about 450 million people were living under communistic dictatorships in the Soviet Union and Asia. He went on to say that the threat is spreading to what was formerly called "Indochina" and could spread like "falling dominoes" to Japan, Formosa (Taiwan), the Philippines, and even Australia and New Zealand.*

[2] *After Kennedy was elected president, the confrontation with the Soviet Union escalated due to the Cuban Missile Crisis. The whole world held its breath as the two superpowers threatened nuclear war. After defusing this crisis, President Kennedy sent "Military Advisors" (MAs) to South Vietnam. Our MAs were supposed to assist the South Vietnamese democratic government against the insurgent Viet Cong (VC), who were threatening to overthrow it in support of communistic North Vietnam.*

2
Moving to Southern California

As I lay upon that gurney at base camp, my thoughts continued to drift to LaGrange and that deep, unsettling feeling of leaving my home for an unknown future in Southern California. That sultry Saturday morning in August of 1954, I remember the smiles and tears mixed upon the faces of my aunts, uncles, and grandparents as we pulled away in my father's 1949 Chevrolet. They disappeared in the distance, along with my home and baseball field—both sources and palettes for my 11-year-old imagination—leaving behind a pale, ghastly impression in my mind that became a reminder of one of the saddest days of my life.

Sensing the tension of the moment, Dad began telling us all that we were taking what he called, "Our Great Adventure." He ended by saying, "If you don't like California, or if it doesn't work out, we can always come back home to LaGrange."

Dad always considered LaGrange home, so I believed if I didn't like it in California, I felt secure knowing we could always come back home. My mom said we'd love California, and knowing my love of baseball, she pointed out that the weather in California was so great that I could play baseball all year long. While those were magical words to my ears, at that moment, I was still very homesick.

As the golden sea of waving wheat of the plain states faded in the distance, the color of the landscape changed to vibrant red dirt, which dad told us was the red clay of Oklahoma. He explained that the tall wooden structures in the distance were oil derricks, and they looked like a manmade forest. The bright red clay seemed to stand out even more because of the black, gummy substance around most of them.

"We're in oil country," Dad said. "Each of those oil derricks is a well."

"What are those green metal things bobbing up and down? They look like giant steel grasshoppers!" I said.

"They're pumps that pull the oil from underground," he replied. "If we owned just one of those wells, we'd be rich. That's what they call, 'black gold.' All of the machines throughout our country use oil. Even the gas that's in our car comes from oil, and it may've even come from one of those very wells."

Neither my sisters nor I knew it at the time, but we were getting more than a history lesson. We were learning that even things far away could affect the simplicity of our lives.

The thunderstorm we passed through in Texas was very frightening, and one I'll never forget. We had plenty of thunderstorms in LaGrange, but the one in Texas was awesome. We actually drove right into it. We could see the looming black clouds ahead, and as we got closer, the wind escalated and moved our loaded car. The scary part was the lightning and thunder, I thought a lightning bolt would strike us for sure, and I'd never see LaGrange or our family again.

First, after the lightning, it started to sprinkle, and as we continued down the highway, the rain came harder and harder, and then it began to hail. I don't think I ever saw it rain so hard, until the monsoon season in Vietnam. After what seemed like forever, we finally saw the sun, and my dad mentioned to my mom that it was quite a rainstorm. I think both of my parents were relieved that it was over, and we had gotten through it okay.

As I turned and looked out the back window to see the black clouds moving away, I told everyone to look back to see the gorgeous rainbow that seemed to be following us. Mom, seizing the opportunity to make the best out of everything, said, "That's God's sign of showing us the way to go, and that the best lay ahead." My dad laughed and asked my mom if she could see the pot of gold.

After leaving Texas and crossing into New Mexico, we could see in the distance the southern range of the Rocky Mountains with its snowcapped peaks. Dad said we didn't have anything like them in LaGrange or Chicago. The view was like a scene out of a western movie, and I imagined myself on a horse, fighting with the outlaws and Indians, just like John Wayne or Roy Rogers.

I remember New Mexico particularly well. We stopped briefly in Gallup, learning it was the "Indian Capital of America," and we saw a number of Indian tribes dancing and selling items along the streets. It was the first time I saw an American Indian, and I wondered how far away Hop-a-Long Cassidy or Gene Autry could be. I didn't realize it at the time, but we were actually heading to where all those western movies were produced and where my childhood heroes really lived. Little did I know that I would one day meet John Wayne and Gene Autry personally and live just a few miles from their homes.

Dad mentioned the "painted desert" as we drove through what was a very desolate area in Arizona, and I think we all said a little prayer that our car wouldn't break down in the middle of nowhere. What I remember most about Arizona is that it was hot—*damn hot*. It got hot in LaGrange, but not this hot, and our car was on the verge of overheating. At the time, I didn't think Dad was using his best judgment, dragging his family through the desert in the middle of the summer and during the hottest part of the day. Even though all the windows were rolled down to catch as much air as possible, I'd say it was like sitting next to a blast furnace.

We stopped at a little place to get gas and something to drink. Dad mentioned to Mom that the thermometer hanging above the counter read 112 degrees—in the shade. As it approached evening, we stayed in a little motel in Phoenix. It did not have air conditioning, but it did have a pool. The pool saved us. Dad told us that we'd be in California the next day, and I couldn't wait—I wasn't alone in that thought.

The next morning, we got on the road early, and already it was hot, so my strongest memory of Arizona was, "Who wants to live here?" Years later, I would change my mind about Arizona when I played winter baseball there. On the start of our fourth day, we finally passed the "Welcome to California" sign on the Arizona border. I noticed that California looked the same as Arizona and nothing like I imagined.

"If this is how Southern California looks," I thought, "it is certainly not a place to play baseball. Who'd ever heard of playing baseball in a desert?"

"Well, even though we are now in California," my father explained, "we are going through the Mojave Desert—America's largest desert." Around noon, it was equally as hot as it had been in Arizona. There was a long stretch where all you could see was white sand and little to no vegetation. Again, we were concerned that our old Chevy would overheat, but we made it through and eventually started to see some signs of life.

Once we saw some rustic houses and cabins, the greenery slowly increased until we finally saw trees—palm trees—which were unlike anything I had seen on the forest preserve. In the late afternoon, we reached my aunt's house and our Long Beach destination. We stayed for one night, and since her house was too small for all of us, we moved to a motel on the Pacific Ocean's shores for a few weeks. Although we had rivers and lakes around LaGrange, the icy waters of Lake Michigan remained the largest body of water I'd ever seen. That is, until I saw the monstrous waves of the Pacific. After the excruciating desert drive, nothing was more inviting.

My dad was an excellent swimmer. In fact, he was such a strong swimmer that he became a hero in LaGrange. He was credited with saving a number of lives—including three children—during a spring flood when their boat capsized in the local river. My dad, my sister Pat, and I took advantage of this time to visit the beach on a daily basis and test the biggest and strongest waves any of us had ever seen.

We actually stayed in Long Beach a few months. While we were at the beach, which was almost daily, we'd walk down to the Rainbow Pier or to a nearby amusement park called "The Pike."

The Pike had all sorts of rides, including a big wooden rollercoaster called "Cyclone Racer," and when you rode it, you thought the speed and the wind were going to send you right into the ocean. This was the first time any of us had ever gone on such a fast ride, and we loved every minute of it.

While staying in Long Beach, my parents enrolled me in Stevenson Elementary School, just six blocks from our motel. Each day, I would walk there and back, but I knew we would be moving soon, so I really didn't take the time to make many friends. The newness of every experience imprinted all these memories firmly into my mind. I was going to a different school, meeting new kids, living in a different city and state, and beginning to adjust to different weather. Although the time we spent there actually seems like a mere instant today, my memories of that period as a family are some of the happiest I've ever known.

It was during our stay in Long Beach that my parents began searching for a place to call home, and they found it in the tiny town of Garden Grove. In 1954, Garden Grove was a sleepy little community southeast of Long Beach in Orange County. Local papers were calling it one of the fastest growing communities in the nation only two years later. None of us realized the explosion in population that would occur in Orange County from that point. Much of it was due to the great weather, an abundance of flat land, and a man named Walt Disney.

When we moved in, orange groves and bean fields dominated the landscape. We also started to add new terms to our vocabulary such as "tract homes" (new homes constructed in a few months that all looked alike). "Freeways" were also a new term that developed into a household word. We had tollways in the Chicago area, but nothing as smooth as these superhighways. Since my father had been a trucker since leaving the service, he felt that this setup would allow him to work more locally and spend more time with his family. After a while, though, he learned that what he thought was a perfect transportation system was also the most congested, nightmarish roadway in the world. My mother feared the freeways, saying, "You really take your life in your hands just trying to get on or off of one." Being from a small town, the hectic speeds worried her.

A music revolution also began in 1954. Bill Haley and the Comets recorded "Rock Around the Clock," and the term "rock and roll" was born. I remember seeing the movie *Blackboard Jungle* and hearing that song. Although my parents didn't care for rock and roll music, it became the sound of my generation and remains so today. I still get a kick remembering that I used to catch them humming some of the popular songs of the time, though. It was just two years later that Elvis Presley changed the music world forever. Although I never considered myself a singer, some told me that I could do a great impersonation of The King. Later in life, and with a few too many beers in me, I'd get together with some of my high school buddies and imitate Elvis singing "Don't Be Cruel"; but you'd never catch me doing that sober!

Mom was right about one thing—the weather in Southern California was ideal. I could play baseball all year long, and to me, that was a dream come true.

Shortly after moving to Garden Grove, Mom signed me up to play little league. I played little league in LaGrange, but this different. During this experience, I could really see the advantages of being tall, and I know it helped when I played little league. My little league coach in Garden Grove was "Whitey" Supernaw—a tall, lanky man, who had played semi-pro baseball. He taught me many of the basics and was an all-around great guy. He was also the first man outside of my grandpa and uncle to really take time with me, and he worked hard to make me a better player.

What I remember most about my first season in California was that Whitey always seemed happy. Perhaps it was due to our spotless record. He let me pitch and play a variety of positions, and I learned to hit from both sides of the plate. Because the league was new, we missed some important deadlines, so we were unable to play in the little league playoffs. We had an awesome team, though, and I think we could have gone a long way. I pitched most of our games, averaged 16 strikeouts per game, and as I mentioned, we had a perfect season. Playing that first season with Coach Whitey is one time that I'll never forget; and I'll always thank him for much of the success I had then and later in baseball.

One thing I missed about being back in LaGrange was watching the baseball games on television with Grandpa Bill. During the summer, I did follow his team, the Chicago Cubs. Unfortunately, they ended that season and many others very near the bottom. In fact, they won just 64 of 154 games that season. I knew Grandpa Bill was disappointed, and I could just hear him saying—as he did years before—"Well . . . there's always next year."

The 1954 World Series was still something. First, I was happy that the Yankees were not in it, and the Cleveland Indians were representing the American League for the first time since they won the World Series in 1948. In '54, Cleveland had a super year, winning 111 games. The New York Giants represented the national league, and a fiery character named Leo Durocher managed them. His team had managed 97 wins to capture the pennant. Yet, in my mind, the Giants were special because of their centerfielder—a man who captured the magic of baseball more than any other had. His name, of course, is Willie Mays. Ted Williams even admitted, "They *invented* the All-Star game for Willie Mays."

The Indians were heavy favorites because of their winning record and boasted some of the best pitchers in baseball. Bob Lemon, Early Wynn, and Mike Garcia were considered the top three pitchers in the American League. They also had plenty of offensive power in their lineup—guys like Larry Doby, who hit 32 homers to lead the league that year. At the end of his career, he became the first black player from the American League elected to the Baseball Hall of Fame.

Because television, and particularly televised sports, was not what it is today, I listened to the game on the radio during school in Garden Grove. Hearing the broadcast of that infamous World Series was interesting since it was supposed to be a one-sided, David-and-Goliath mismatch—and it turned out to be just that. The story played out the same way as the Biblical account—except, in this case, David was a Giant, and his team was from New York. The mighty Indians fell in a four-game sweep that became one of the biggest and most surprising upsets in any sport during the 1950s.

I missed seeing this World Series with Grandpa Bill because we were thousands of miles away from one another. I would have loved to have watched it with him. I know that he was watching it and loving every moment even though the Cubs weren't playing. He dreamed of the day that he'd see me help return the Cubs to what he believed was their rightful place in baseball history as the "Greatest Team in Baseball." Although the Cubs had played in the World Series just five times in 66 years, the real disappointment was they had never won a series. He was sure that I'd make the difference.

Having so much fun playing baseball successfully helped eliminate most of my homesickness, but I still thought about my family and my old baseball field in LaGrange. California and the little town of Garden Grove weren't bad, but I still didn't consider them home. Home was LaGrange, and I knew if things didn't work out, that's where we would be going—and that was fine with me. However, as time passed, LaGrange and my boyhood home began to fade in my mind, just the way it had as I looked out the rear window of our car the day we left. A new house and many new friends in California helped contribute to making LaGrange more of a fond memory instead of a backup destination. With the on-field success I was enjoying and the ideal weather for playing the game I loved most, Garden Grove, California, was beginning to feel more like home.

The new home my parents bought was in a middle-class neighborhood. All the homes in the area were new, and as a result, we came to know our neighbors, and there were many neighborhood get-togethers. Seemingly, most of our neighborhood had made the exodus to California from the Midwest, and that helped to smooth the adjustment. As Mom often said, "We've met more people and made more friends than ever before!" The people and the beautiful weather added to our enjoyment, and with everyone truly liking our new home, there seemed to be less talk each day about going back to LaGrange.

Since most pastimes took place outdoors in Southern California, one of our favorite family activities was going to the drive-in to see movies. *On the Waterfront*, starring Marlon Brando, seems to stand out more than others when I think back. Pat, my sister, and my mom felt that Brando was the most talented and handsome actor on the silver screen. In this role, he portrayed a down-and-out dockworker who, due to unfortunate circumstances, had to forsake his professional boxing career. I recall thinking that the movie was sad because he never realized his dream in life. Although I couldn't identify with such disappointment at that time, we all learn dreams can be denied at any time.

While our family was trying to adjust to our new home, Pat immediately became one of the most popular girls in the neighborhood. My mother used to say, "Your sister has more friends than Carter has pills." Pat really took to California, and as I mentioned earlier, she loved the beach. I'm sure if you ask her today, she would call herself a "true California girl."

Through the years, she and my mom were the ones in our family who kept in touch and visited with our relatives in both LaGrange (Dad's side) and Maywood, Illinois (Mom's side). My mom shared Pat's love of California, and over the years, I soon shared that sentiment as well. My younger sister, Cathy, truly is a California girl. I doubt if she ever considered herself anything but being from California, and today she and her husband own a successful catering service and real estate business in central California. I am grateful and pleased that both she and Pat did keep in contact with our relatives in LaGrange and Maywood, and now, looking back over the years, I regret not doing a better job with that.

When I began school in Garden Grove, I was introduced to more kids who would become friends. In LaGrange, there weren't that many kids, so now I was meeting more than ever before. At first, because I am somewhat shy, I was fearful of going to school. Not knowing what to expect can create some anxiety, but after the first day, all of that uncertainty was gone.

Part of the initial problem was that my sister Pat and I had always gone to school together, but being three years older, she now attended junior high school, while I was going to elementary school at a different location. Because of this, we didn't even take the same school bus or leave or get home at the same time, so I was really on my own that first day and quite nervous. Because I had met some of the neighbor kids before school began, seeing their faces at the bus stop and talking to them on the bus broke the ice and made the transition painless.

Going to school in 1954 was somewhat surreal to me. I remember the teacher having us practice "duck and cover drills," in which we were all told to get under our desk and hide our eyes in case we had an atomic bomb dropped on us. We'd never done this in LaGrange, and at the time, I thought it was all very silly.

When I got home, I asked Pat if they had those drills, but she said they hadn't. Later, she said they had begun drills in her school as well. This was the first time that I was exposed to a real, perceived danger, and as a result, I started thinking about the possibility of being blown to bits. While I never really took those drills seriously, I definitely did not enjoy hearing about them or discussing the topic. I don't think I was ever truly afraid that it might happen, but, the newscasts on television and the radio were always talking about a Cold War with the Soviet Union. We learned in school that, if we ever did have a World War III, it would be fought with nuclear weapons and destroy everything.

In the early and mid-1950s the news was about the Cold War, the Soviet Union, and their communist government. The McCarthy Hearings were in the news, causing a substantial concern that communists were already among us and even in high places in our own government. The height of this scare came in 1954, when a national poll showed that 78 percent of Americans believed it was important to report relatives and acquaintances suspected of being communists to the FBI.

All of this propaganda spawned a simple question in my mind:

"Mom, what does a 'communist' look like?"

She laughed, of course, saying, "They look like most people, Roy, except they don't like America and what we stand for."

"Do we know anyone who is a communist?" I recall asking.

"I've never met any," she replied with a comforting smile. "You shouldn't be concerned about that anyway."

Ironically, just 14 years later, I was fighting and killing communists in Vietnam, and they were trying to kill me and everyone else with whom I served.

The biggest story in 1954 actually had nothing to do with the communists or the Cold War. *Brown v. the Board of Education*, a landmark Supreme Court case involved black children, their parents, and a public high school in Kansas. The Supreme Court struck down the "separate but equal" doctrine that kept the races separate in schools— one practiced in this country for close to a century. The Supreme Court decision sent shock waves throughout the country, and I remember our family, friends, and neighbors had strongly differing points of view at times—views so strong that many communities rioted, setting in motion a decade of civil rights protests and unrest.

How did this landmark decision affect me? At the time, it had little effect on me personally, because through my years in public school, I never had a black student in any of my classes. After that decision, nothing changed; I still did not have any in my school classes. That's not to say I didn't compete against some black kids in sports—I did and found that they were as competitive as anyone else was. Being from a white family in a white, middle-class neighborhood, I really didn't understand the problem or concern. As the years passed, however, I did see prejudice and learned that the playing field and the opportunity for blacks was anything but equal.

I didn't realize it at the time, but the 1950s would provide many of my fondest memories. Families could live, for the most part, on one parent's income; there were no major wars; and compared to what I see today, we were insulated more from conflict. In some respects, life mirrored the television show *Happy Days*.

Speaking of television, that little box became the biggest communication invention of the century. Television was in its infancy, and some say that the 1950s marked its "Golden Age." Mom's favorite program was *I Love Lucy*, while the shows I enjoyed the most were *The Twilight Zone* and *The Rifleman* starring Chuck Connors. I remember when the movie studios feared that television would ultimately kill the movie business because it was believed people would prefer to stay home and not go to the movies. It's interesting that just the opposite has happened.

A similar fear existed that televising sporting events would keep people from buying tickets to baseball games and other sporting events. I was even a little concerned about it. Again, history showed the opposite happened. Television created even more interest, and attendance at the ballparks of America continued to grow.

The benefit of all this television exposure actually increased the revenue for all professional sports organizations. Today's teams, owners, and players receive so much revenue from television that the average salary for most players is in the millions—a far cry from what they were in the 1950s, or even when I was playing. I remember when players during the 1950s had to get jobs during the off-season just to pay rent.

I realized for the first time during 1954 that my life had changed. It became a time of new explorations, a time of more immediate family togetherness and difficulties. It also was the time that I experienced tremendous highs, or as I like to think of it, "top-of-the-mountain happiness," and some of the lowest, or bottom-of-the-gorge lows, in family disappointment and sadness. In short, as the Bible and the song say, " . . .to every thing there is a season and a time to every purpose under the sun."

During that "season under the sun," while my life had changed, so too had our nation and the world. President Eisenhower gave his famous "Dominoes" speech, and established our financial and military support for South Vietnam. The "Domino Theory" became a part of our foreign policy. Later that year, Eisenhower wrote a letter to the president of South Vietnam, promising more support for the country. Ironically, it was 14 years later when that decision and my future would collide.

A major U.S. highway system was being planned in 1954 as well. Dad, being in the trucking business, told us that would be good for business and possibly justified our move to California. The program would cost five billion dollars per year for the next 10 years, with emphasis being on constructing a network of interstate and intercity highways. At the time this program was announced, 70 percent of American families owned a car. When enacted, it became the largest public works venture in American history. Dad was concerned about how such a program would be funded, but at the same time, he knew trucking could replace railroads in moving freight, and trucking was his livelihood.

One other thought comes to mind about 1954. President Eisenhower signed a congressional resolution changing the pledge of allegiance. The two words, "under God," were inserted, changing the words to " . . . one nation, under God, indivisible. . . ." It didn't really matter to me, because I believe in God, and I suppose to have God's blessing on our country is a good thing. To those who do not believe in God, this did become an important issue. I recall that many felt this violated the "separation of church and state" clause in the Constitution.

In 1954, many changes occurred for me, and I felt most of them would work out well. Unfortunately, not all of our family was as happy as I was about calling Garden Grove, California, "home." I didn't realize the seriousness of what was about to happen, but soon something would change our family forever and have a profound affect on all of us—including my life and career.

3
Dad Went Out to Make a Phone Call

Perhaps my youth prohibited me from picking up the important signals that, over many months, would later change my life forever. After several weeks in that Long Beach motel, we were all getting on each other's nerves. When we finally received the call that our new home in Garden Grove was ready, everyone was ready to move. Of course, the home was a ranch-style house, and I remember my mom thinking that the term, "California ranch-style home," sounded romantic. My dad thought it was nothing but a sales pitch. Mom raved about the new kitchen; Dad thought the yard was too small, but that would be my responsibility anyway, since he'd be on the road most of the time. Dad thought the neighbors were too close, and he hated the idea of fenced yards. Mom liked the idea; her neighbors were less than a mile away, and she was pleased that her in-laws didn't surround her. She liked the idea of meeting new people and doing things with other families. She thought the yard and the neighborhood were perfect.

From my point of view, I agreed with my father about the yard—it was much too small. I was used to having a space big enough for my own baseball field, but I could barely have an infield in Garden Grove. I was also leery of strangers being on all sides and so close. Of course, I hated the yard work as well—it always seemed to interrupt my fun.

Dad insisted that it be done, though—and I couldn't pacify him with a simple, "I'll do it, Dad."

"Roy, you told me you would do the yard work!" He'd yell in his generally foul mood. "When did you plan to do it?"

"In a little while. . . ."

"No!" He'd reply in a very firm tone. "Do it now—and I mean, 'now!' No more playing until it's done!"

The work was disturbing for me, particularly because I couldn't play in baseball games until it was finished. He explained that he was teaching me responsibility and the reality of "work." Yet, I began to hate that yard and even resent him. I felt that since he didn't care much for sports or baseball, he was keeping me from pursuing my dream. In reality, though, he did teach me responsibility—if you had a job to do, you couldn't play around or have fun until it was done. His legacy is that I carry that work ethic to this day.

As time went on, I thought we all were adjusting to our new life and new location, but there was one irritation on which we had all agreed. We missed having a telephone. We didn't know it at the time, but this little town of Garden Grove was exploding in growth. The boom in population had slowed the phone company's ability to supply the demand. We had to wait three months until a phone was installed. My parents liked to call Illinois frequently and they didn't like to brave all kinds of weather to make their long-distance calls. Also, since our friends and family couldn't call us either, the lack of that little convenience soon developed into a major headache.

On another note, I remember going to several elementary schools that year, again because the community was outgrowing the number of classrooms available. This, of course, made it very difficult for me to make friends because I was being shipped between schools, teachers, and classrooms; but my mother assured us that it would all come together soon enough.

We enjoyed our first Christmas in California that year together as a family, and, while I had no idea at that time, there would only be one more occasion that we'd share that experience. Instead of snow and ice, we had warm weather and sunshine, and I could go outside and play with the new baseball and bat I received. I also received a new baseball glove, which was really special. I remember both my uncles and grandpa would say, "When you get a new glove you need to 'break it in' by putting neadsfoot oil on it to keep the leather from cracking."

I remember rubbing that glove hard with the oil to conform it to my hand. I think my dad thought I was crazy, but, as I mentioned, he didn't care that much for baseball. Had I been putting oil in a model truck engine, he would've probably been much happier. He might have even sat down beside me, feeling that I was a chip off the old block. Even then, we had very little in common.

That particular Christmas day was all baseball for me. After all, I thought the weather was the reason we came to California. As far as I was concerned, I was here so I could spend most of that day outside with all of my tools (my baseball bat and glove), loving every minute of it.

That first Christmas day in Garden Grove, California, was far different from the 11 that I spent in LaGrange. As the sun started to set, I thought about my grandpa and uncle and wondered what they were doing. Sure, I missed them, my baseball field, the beauty of a "white Christmas," and countryside in LaGrange, but the warm sun of California and the chance to play baseball all year long were winning me over. I could tell that my dad missed his family and LaGrange. Although I don't recall him saying that directly to me, I picked up on that from some of the things he'd say to my mom.

That Christmas was also memorable because of what happened that afternoon. I had long forgotten about it until my mom reminded me of it. At first, she had quite a scare, but later both she and I laughed about it.

In the back yard, we had a large trash barrel into which we threw old papers. Deciding to pack it down, I jumped on top of the papers and ended up getting wedged inside the barrel. My mom called for me to come in, and when I didn't, she went looking for me. As she continued to call, I replied, and she became frantic when she could hear my response but couldn't see me. Finally, she traced my yelps to the barrel and tried to help me, but she couldn't get me out, and that's when I started to become concerned. She called my dad, and he and some neighbors, who had come over by now to see what all the yelling was about, came to the rescue. At first, everybody was laughing, but after a considerable amount of tugging and pulling, they finally got me out of the barrel. We all laugh about it today, but at the time, I was positive I'd spend my final Christmas wedged into a trash barrel.

Our first year in California was really a time for adjustment. The biggest adjustment for my sisters and me was to make new friends at a new school. For my mother, making new friends was a primary transition as well. Because she was friendly, her adjustment seemed to be the easiest. I may not have fully realized that her relationship with my dad seemed strained at times. Dad was more like a duck out of water. The thing he liked most about Southern California was the weather. He didn't like the idea of having to get up in the morning to walk outside into a cold and cloudy Midwestern snowstorm and shovel snow so he could get his truck out of the driveway. However, he did say he missed the four seasons, and I could see in his eye that LaGrange was still home to him, and he missed it far more than we did.

My father left the house to "make a phone call," as my mother told us, just six months after our second Christmas. Since he didn't pack a suitcase, take any of his clothes or important items, and because Mom or Pat was always using the phone, I accepted that story. As it turned out, he didn't return for over a year. His absence wasn't unusual—he was a truck driver, and he was often gone for long periods. Yet, after a few weeks, I became quite concerned, and my mom—rather than sitting down with each of us to reveal the truth—kept telling us that he'd be returning soon.

After several months, my mother finally told us that he had gone back to LaGrange because he couldn't find suitable work in California. She said he wanted to go back to where he knew more people and could find a better job. Although I had spent many years without my father's constant presence, I was very disappointed that he wouldn't let my sisters and me know that he was leaving or why. Since I felt, at the time, that that was a terrible way to treat his family, my perception of my father changed.

Honestly, I had always looked up to my dad. He was a hero to me. He was a war veteran, and Grandpa Bill had told me about a day when my father saved nine people—including three children—from drowning in the Des Plaines and Skokie Rivers. My father was 21 at the time. Over an Easter holiday, he had saved six adults and a 14-month-old baby when their boat capsized in one river. The very next day, he saved two more young boys who were caught in the other river's fast-moving current. My grandpa saved clippings from the local newspapers and proudly showed them to me when I was young. I still have them. At the time, I shared his pride and my mother's faith in my father's courage and sense of self-sacrifice in the face of danger.

That hero and my father walked out hand in hand when he abandoned us in California. He didn't write, and while he knew that we finally had a phone, he didn't call. To my knowledge, he didn't send any money to pay for anything. I couldn't understand how he could do that to his wife and children.

My father's departure left a veil of sadness over our home. Many nights I could hear my mother crying herself to sleep and would wonder in angst how he could do this to her. How did his leaving affect me? My mother informed me that I'd now be "the man of the house," and that I'd have to be strong. Was it traumatic and life changing? Of course it was.

I kept going over the same questions in my mind. "Okay, so the bastard's gone, and he has left his family and all his obligations—now what do we do?" I was in junior high. I wasn't a man yet. I knew that I couldn't undertake the responsibility of supporting my mother and sisters. I remember telling myself that baseball was the answer. If I worked really hard at what I excelled in, perhaps I'd be able to do it. I promised Mom and myself that I'd forget about his abandonment. I'd make it in baseball, play in the major leagues, and take care of her and our family.

Truthfully, I was pissed because of what he'd done to all of us. He seemed more like a coward than the hero that my grandpa introduced into my imagination just years before. I envied my friends whose fathers would be cheering them on at our baseball games. Where was mine? He didn't care about baseball before, but now I felt like he didn't care about us, either. I don't think he ever recognized my interest or abilities, and that always bothered me. Looking back today, I can understand some of his thinking there. He probably considered playing professional baseball to be an impossible dream. Maybe he felt that by learning a trade, I would be better off in the end. Yet his indifference truly bothered me. When I'd come home from a game, he'd never ask me how I had done or if we had won. I began to figure that baseball was nothing more to him than a waste of time.

As a result, I began to think of guys such as Whitey Supernaw as more of a father to me than my own. At least Whitey would encourage me, and he went home after each game to his own family—he didn't run out on them as my father did.

Of course, as in many unfortunate domestic situations, my father's leaving was bittersweet. On one hand, I didn't have a father around to advise me and enjoy my athletic successes. On the other hand, my mother allowed me much more freedom than he would have, and that helped me to develop a sense of responsibility and maturity faster than most of my friends.

Every boy needs a father—not just a biological connection to someone, either, but someone who will love his children and raise a young man to do the same. A boy needs someone to encourage him to do better when things aren't going well and let him know that he'll be there when problems arise. I missed having a real "father" in my life, but as some might say, times were different. His abandonment fired my desire to play baseball, and that day may have been the catalyst that got me into professional baseball many years later. In my life, I hope I don't disappoint my children, and I want to be there when they need me. I realize that they need the freedom to think for themselves and choose their own paths. I want them to know that I will never abandon them.

Although my father's abandonment overwhelms every memory that I have from that era, I do recall many other important events taking place around that time. Our country started sending "military advisors" to South Vietnam to counsel that country's armed forces. We were told that Americans would not be sent into active combat with or without Vietnamese troops. Where was that directive 13 years later?

The Brooklyn Dodgers had just defeated the Yankees in the World Series, clinching the championship in a riveting Game 7 victory. The Dodgers, who had just won their first championship in eight previous attempts, relied on defense and the shutout pitching of Johnny Podres to claim the title. Walter Alston, in only his second year as the Dodgers manager, was propelled into the high favor of Brooklyn management and fans. Although I was only 12 at the time, I knew someday that I'd be out there. Along with Grandpa Bill, I hoped it'd be for the Cubs— the greatest team in baseball. That sentiment would change soon, though.

I remember taking some odd jobs to help out with our overhead— most of them petty tasks for a couple bucks. Although that's very little by today's standards, it was much more than my father had ever paid me for work, and Congress had just raised the minimum wage from $0.75 to $1.00 per hour. I entered junior high with much more to consider in life than a normal 12-year-old. I met a teacher who would help me with that, though. Mr. Mann, my physical education teacher and baseball coach, remains prevalent in my mind today—almost 45 years later. He was the first teacher and coach who really took the time to work with me individually, and that influence gave me great confidence at a crucial time in my development as a player and a young man. Baseball also revealed its financial rewards around that time. As our coach, Mr. Mann would reward home runs with quarters that we could use for malts. That incentive paid off, as I hit many home runs and downed a ton of those malts—thank God, I was growing like a weed, so I never put on any weight! Even today, when I have a malt, I can still see Mr. Mann's smiling face. Mr. Mann, wherever you are today, I'll never forget you for your kindness and for rebuilding confidence.

By the summer of 1956, I was no longer eligible to play little league—I had graduated to Babe Ruth Baseball. For the first time, I'd be playing with 90-foot base paths and a professional pitching mound. Luckily, I had prepared for this transition when I was living in LaGrange, for this is how I modeled my private baseball field as a child. For the first time, I'd be able to utilize my speed and steal some bases. It was also the first time that I'd be allowed to wear spikes.

Luckily, I had Whitey as my coach again, and we had one of the better teams in the league. I really felt like I was finally playing "real" baseball. We led off, stole bases, pitched from the stretch, picked off potential base thieves, learned about the balk—everything like the pros. Although I had pitched in little league, I primarily threw fastballs and changeups. I began to learn the curveball, and I tried to master it throughout the season. Although I seldom used it (I didn't want to injure my developing arm), I felt like a "real" pitcher. I'll never forget that first season, but there were two events that I happened during one game that I'll never forget:

For one, I threw my first no-hitter that season. What made it more special, however, was that my father was there to see the game. After leaving us so abruptly, I was shocked to see him sitting in the stands. Secondly, the joy was short-lived, though, as he left halfway through the game. For whatever reason, he missed seeing me complete my first no-hitter. I was devastated. I acted like it didn't matter, but it did, of course. After a while, though, I thought, "Why should I be surprised? He's never been there before; so why should I expect him to be here now?" Overall, I think it toughened me emotionally. I understand now that we each have a life to lead, but it would've been nice if my father could've stayed to see me finish an accomplishment of which I was so proud. Perhaps I just wanted him to show that he was proud of me, too. I'll never forget the day I pitched my first no-hitter was also the last time I'd see my father for many years.

I remember that game being outdone, though, by one slightly better. In the 1956 World Series, the Yankees were once again facing the Dodgers. Although the Yankees won the Series in seven games, Game 5 became a piece of history. Yankee right-handed starting pitcher Don Larsen threw the first and only perfect game ever in a World Series. He faced the minimum of 27 batters and threw just 97 pitches to capture the win.

During this time, baseball and my love for the game maintained my interest and probably kept me out of trouble.

I remember one of my teachers asking, "Roy, what do you want to do when you're finished with school?"

"I want to play professional baseball," I answered.

She smiled, and asked, "Are you planning to play baseball your entire life?"

"If I could, I would," I said proudly. The class laughed aloud in unison. "I'm not sure what I'll do when I'm too old for that, but I'm definitely planning on playing baseball for as long as I can."

Although my answer may have seemed childish, I was quite serious. However, I did realize that day that I'd have to do something else with my life—when I was done playing, of course. I hoped that I could stay involved with the game, even later in life, by being a coach or a scout.

Fate is a very mysterious phenomenon. In 1957, the National League approved the proposed move of the Dodgers and Giants from New York to California. The Giants would move to San Francisco, and the Dodgers would move to Los Angeles. For the first time in baseball history, two major league ball teams would be located on the West Coast, and one of them would be only 30 miles from my home. A dream came true; this would be my chance, and I felt like my prayers had been heard. My destiny had been set into motion.

Of course, the jubilation of West Coast fans was overwhelmed only by the immediate vacancy felt in New York. The city had lost their Giants, who had left the hallowed Polo Grounds for Seals Stadium in San Francisco; and their beloved "Bums," who left empty echoes in Ebbets field for the Coliseum in Los Angeles. All part of baseball's growing pains, both teams were lured by the "gold out west." The Los Angeles Dodgers became a reality in 1958, playing their first game against the Giants. The excitement began with a parade marching to the

Los Angeles Coliseum—supposedly named and designed to resemble the Roman Coliseum, even though it wasn't designed with baseball in mind. A public referendum was soon passed—albeit barely. No longer would the team have to maintain the 100,000-seat facility designed for the Olympics and football.

For the first time in my life, I was torn between the love Grandpa Bill and I shared for the Chicago Cubs and the new Major League Baseball team that had come to town—the Los Angeles Dodgers. As time passed and circumstances changed, my choice for my favorite team would not be that difficult to make. Perhaps it would have been different if my dad had been there to advise or counsel me, but he wasn't; and subconsciously, I probably resented that fact anyway.

Although I was not aware of it at the time, the Los Angeles Dodgers did something that was quite smart. Recognizing that Southern California was perhaps the best market in America for baseball talent, they wanted to capitalize on that market. They decided to hold tryouts for young players—17 years or older, mostly top high school or community college prospects—who would like to play for the Dodger Rookies. Word spread through newspaper stories and letters to coaches. The response was overwhelming, and the Dodgers found hundreds of kids answered the call. No other major league team at that time, especially in the Southern California area, was doing this; and as a result, many of those unsigned Rookies became future Dodgers. Not only that, but by playing other amateur teams around the state, it was also great public relations for the Dodgers and their youth baseball program.

I began high school in 1958, but just before the baseball season, I broke my left arm fooling around at my friend's house. Do you think I'd let a broken arm stand in my way of playing baseball and realizing my dream? No way—even with my cast, I pitched junior varsity that year. Until the cast was off, our catcher would throw the ball to our third baseman (Jan Martin) after each pitch, and he'd walk over and hand me the ball. Unbelievable, but that's what we did, and we won most of our games. Jan later played in the Dodger organization, and after baseball, became a very successful businessman. Today he's retired, and we still keep in touch.

By 1958, many conflicts had developed in my personal life and in the world at large. At 15, I hadn't seen my father for over 18 months, and my family was barely managing financially. However, I was entering high school and my first season playing American Legion baseball. At that time, Legion ball was the most competitive league one could be a part of, and I loved every minute of it.

The disappointment that I felt over my father's leaving, was as I stated before, devastating to my mom, sisters, and me. However, the truth would be revealed to us many years later. My sisters and I went through a storage facility, and we all found that we'd been misled for most of our lives. We learned that my dad indeed had attempted to contact us on several occasions. He had sent cards, letters, and money from every paycheck, but my mother, for a number of reasons—most likely because she was hurt—denied my dad had sent anything, keeping the truth from us. Although I don't agree with what she did, I have come to understand it. She saw that I was adjusting to his absence and thought she was doing the right thing. She thought that it would just add more problems. To her, he didn't want to be an active participant in our lives. However, I'm pleased that I learned about this and had a chance to talk to my dad after many years. I'm particularly pleased that we had a chance to set the record straight before he passed away. It was important to know that he hadn't abandoned his family and that he did try to contact us. He was human, and mistakes were made on both sides.

4

Meeting a Man Named Myers

W ith jet-black hair and a cigar always in mouth or hand, the short, stocky man stands tall in my mind—even today.

Jim Muhe introduced me to Kenny Myers when I was just 15 years old while I was playing American Legion ball. Jim was a "birddog," which is what, in those days some called scouts who lacked the authority to sign ballplayers. Jim came to our games, and he'd watch me play for a while. Apparently he was impressed by my abilities, which led him to tell Kenny about me. Upon Jim's recommendation, Kenny attended a game, where I met him afterward.

Meeting a pro scout was the answer to my prayers and my dreams. He represented my ticket into the big leagues. Prior to meeting Kenny, I'd played junior varsity ball as a freshman and enjoyed a great season, even though I suffered from the aforementioned broken arm. Once the summer of '58 rolled around, the cast was off, and I was ready for Legion ball. I loved the level of competition that I saw each game, and although I was the youngest player on the team, I was taller (six foot two) than many of my teammates and competed for the team lead in batting. For the first time since moving to California, I was mingling with the best ballplayers the area had to offer.

After making the starting rotation, I enjoyed a very good season from the mound, winning most of my games. When I wasn't pitching,

Kenny Myers talks hitting at a restaurant in 1962. *From the Roy Gleason Collection*

I was playing outfield and enjoying a great season at the plate. All of this attracted Jim Muhe, who would speak with me before and after our games. He felt that I had a true future in baseball. All I could think around that time was, "I guess he's telling the truth if he's bringing Kenny Myers," who was one of the top scouts for the Los Angeles Dodgers.

My final three years at Garden Grove High School were filled with highlight moments. During that period, I pitched four no-hitters, many one-hitters, and came very close to pitching a perfect game.

The last game of my senior year, we were winning 1-0, and the team we were playing was unable to get a man aboard. With two outs, I threw a fastball to the hitter, who hit a slow groundball down the third-base line. Our third baseman and I both went for the ball, but we both hesitated when the ball appeared to be rolling foul—but it didn't. By the time it was called "fair," there was no time for the play. Steaming mad, I headed back to the mound and proceeded to blow three of my

ABOVE: Roy's varsity baseball coach at Garden Grove High, Mike Sgobba (left), with Roy in 1961. *From the Roy Gleason Collection*

BELOW: Garden Grove High School varsity baseball team, "The Argonauts," in 1961—Roy is at top center. *From the Roy Gleason Collection*

hardest fastballs past the next hitter for the last out. The previous hitter had earned a hit from the scorer, but I thought it was a fluke.

From 1958 to 1961, I played baseball literally year-round, and I loved every minute. Of course, there were times that I didn't perform as well, and there were times when I would slack a bit in practice—but those instances were few and far between. I was on a mission to become the best baseball player that I could be. I never became burned out. Each day only served to bolster my confidence and love of the game even more. Baseball was my "drug of choice," and I was addicted.

During my four years at Garden Grove High School, I had opportunities to play other sports. Both the football and basketball coaches were always trying to talk me into playing. Each time, I would tell them, "All I want to do is play professional baseball. I'm going to concentrate strictly on that." After a while, they stopped asking and accepted my decision to commit to baseball.

Fortunately, during this period, I had some outstanding baseball coaches in both high school and American Legion. My high school coach was Mike Sgobba, and he was excellent. Although I was his leading hitter, he told me later that he thought my best chance of playing pro ball would be on the mound as a pitcher. During most of my high school playing days, I concentrated on being a great pitcher, but all of that changed when I met Kenny Myers. For two years, Kenny worked with me after school and even during the winter. He asked me to play on the Winter League team that he managed. During the regular school and Legion seasons, he'd attend some of the games, but for the most part, it was a break from each other.

꙳ ꙳ ꙳

As a major scout for the Dodgers, Kenny was credited with discovering a track star from Roosevelt High School who owned the national long-jump record (25 feet, five inches). That kid also played baseball, pitching from the left side and batting from the right. Originally Kenny had scouted him at a track meet but ended up investing hard hours working with this young man. He taught the kid how to bat from the left side, telling him that the switch was critical to his success. In order to take advantage of the kid's speed, Kenny convinced him that he should be in the outfield, not on the mound. After remodeling him, Kenny signed his protégé to a professional contract. That young kid played 18 seasons in the majors and amassed more than 2,500 hits. His name is Willie Davis.

Kenny Myers believed that, if a player had natural athletic ability and great foot speed, he could teach you everything else you needed to know about baseball. That's what elevated him above his colleagues in my mind and allowed him to fish talent out of competitive areas. One just had to learn to make contact with the ball. If you listened and learned, he felt that you could be a pro. Many scouts today may dispute this claim, but Kenny proved it repeatedly, with Willie Davis evidencing his expertise.

I personally witnessed Kenny's abilities as he transformed another athlete with very little baseball experience into a major leaguer. In December of 1959, Omar Kahle, a childhood friend, introduced me to Clarence Jones. Omar had met Clarence at Santa Ana Community College. Clarence was there to play football, and he'd already earned "Little All-American" recognition. After shooting the breeze one day, Clarence told Omar that he wanted to play professional sports, and Omar suggested baseball. When Clarence revealed that he'd love a shot, Omar told him that he had a friend who was working with one of baseball's top scouts—me—and told Clarence that he'd introduce all of us. He brought Omar to my home and asked me to introduce him to Kenny.

Meeting Clarence was a unique experience for various reasons. He was the first black kid I'd ever met—he became a close, dear friend and part of my family. Like me, he'd grown up in the Midwest (Cleveland) and had moved to Southern California just recently. After we got to talking about baseball, I asked if he'd like to play winter league ball with me, and shortly thereafter, I brought him to a game to meet the man named Myers.

Kenny soon realized that Clarence was a true prospect. He thought, with some work, he would have another Willie Davis on his hands. After transforming Clarence into an excellent ballplayer, Kenny signed Clarence to a contract with the Dodgers. Although he went on to enjoy a successful career in the majors, it was not with the Dodgers; but with my grandpa's favorite squad, the Chicago Cubs.

I was able to see firsthand Kenny's innate ability to transform good athletes into major league baseball players. Here's a small list of just some other players whose careers are owed, at least partially, to the man named Myers:

Willie Crawford—12 seasons with the Dodgers and 14 overall.
Dick Nen—One season with the Dodgers and six overall.
Larry Burright—One season with the Dodgers and three overall.
Tim Johnson—Six seasons with Milwaukee and seven overall.

K enny was both a true student of the game and a baseball genius. At 15, he signed a professional contract with the St. Louis Browns—making him one of the youngest players ever to do so. Although he never made it out of the minors, he did play for over 20 years. I believe he even set a record in his day by hitting two grand slams and two more home runs in a single game. When his playing days ended, he stuck to his roots. Instead of seeking a nine-to-five job, he stayed in baseball, becoming a scout with the Dodgers.

Most baseball scouts evaluate talent by assessing the number of tools that a player possesses: arm strength, hitting ability, base speed, and game experience. Kenny was different in that he didn't place much emphasis on experience. He focused on three major areas, the first being foot speed. He felt that "God-given" abilities made the difference between someone who could be good and someone who could be great. Secondly, he noted how skilled a player's hand-eye coordination was and if he could make contact with the ball. If you had this talent, he felt that you could become a good—and possibly great—hitter. He knew that every team was interested in players who could hit the ball out of the park. Lastly, Kenny often asked, "Does this prospect have the heart that it takes to grow into a great ballplayer?" He wanted to see the necessary hunger that it took to become a major leaguer—he wanted to see someone who would forego anything and everything for that chance. If you lacked this ingredient, you were nothing more than a loaf of bread without the yeast.

Unique to his era, Kenny rarely considered signing college graduates. When asked why, he responded, "I'm not against education, but I believe that the majority of the players going through the minors and into the majors will be [and are] those players who 'do not have anything to fall back on.'" He felt that a college degree reminded a player that he didn't need baseball.

"When the going gets tough," he'd explain, "as it does in the minors, the college grad will simply pick up his suitcase and move on. He will not stick it out because he has too many other options that his degree offers."

To my knowledge, Kenny didn't sign any college graduates.

Known as an expert on hitting, Kenny influenced or taught many major league players who later became managers, and coaches; and even today, that influence is evident throughout baseball. He was obsessed with hitting—so much so that practically everything he talked about concerned hitting and how to improve your hitting skill. If you asked him about politics or what was going on in the world, he would just give you a little far-off stare and then smile—but he would voice his opinion about one issue quite adamantly: racial prejudice.

Kenny was not prejudiced, and he probably signed more minority ballplayers than any other scout in that era. He was very vocal in his disgust with the way that blacks were treated in those days. The late 1950s and early 1960s were a time of civil rights protest and racial tension. Every newspaper and television program depicted demonstrations or riots happening somewhere in America. Although

The Dodger Rookies of 1960—Roy, 17, on left; Kenny Myers, center; and Jim Acton. *Courtesy of the Los Angeles Dodgers. All rights reserved.*

Kenny disagreed with the riots, he felt that blacks were being treated unfairly, and that needed to change.

I recall an incident when he was coaching the Dodger Rookies. We left L.A. in the morning for a night game in Bakersfield, and the bus stopped at a roadside restaurant early that afternoon. As we all sat down, we noticed some of the employees were staring at us with bewildered faces. At first, we thought it was because we were the "Dodger Rookies."

As we glanced at the menu, the manager approached Kenny, and said, "I'd be happy to serve everyone except the two black kids."

Kenny stood slowly, stared the manager down, and said, "If you're not serving everyone, we're not eating here."

The manager contritely replied, "I'm sorry, but I can't do that, sir."

"Go to hell. Let's go, guys—back on the bus." Kenny bellowed, and we boarded the bus.

Once aboard, Kenny got all of our attention: "Don't worry, guys. We'll find another restaurant."

We did, and there were no more problems of that sort. I had never witnessed that sort of bigotry before; but on that day, Kenny showed us his true colors and his contempt for that sort of ignorance. All we knew was that he was right.

꿈 꿈 꿈

K enny felt that baseball favored left-handed hitters because they were two steps closer to first base. He'd often ask right-handed hitters, "How many times have you been thrown out by a step or two?"

He'd contend that left-handed hitters hit more home runs, asserted on the evidence that most right-field fences were closer to the plate than left-field fences for the first have of the century. He also knew that most pitchers are right-handed, giving left-handed batters an obvious advantage, such as hitting the curve ball, which curved into your power zone instead of away from it. Although some experts and hitting coaches may dispute these claims today, most of the game's best hitters—including Ty Cobb, Babe Ruth, Ted Williams, and Stan Musial—batted from the left side.

As with many others, Kenny clearly stated from the beginning that he was far more interested in me as hitter than as a pitcher. He didn't have a tough time selling me on this—he knew, above all, I wanted *to play*.

When it came to "God-given" abilities, I was very blessed. I had a strong right arm, ran like the wind, and hit with power from both sides of the plate.

"Kid," Kenny would tell me, "you have all the tools, and I'd like to work with you to sharpen those tools."

Work we did, for hours on end. We'd hit for hours, mostly from the left side, and practice "driving the ball" and "pulling the ball with power." After a day's practice, I was left with more blisters than Kenny had cigars, but to a kid whose dream was playing major league baseball, I couldn't get enough.

He was the first coach to tell me, "You need to swing *down* on a high pitch."

I had never heard that before.

"Roy, imagine yourself pounding a stake into the ground. You don't pound a stake by swinging up at it; you club it down. It's the same way with a high pitch."

After many workouts, I found that he was right, and when I started swinging down, I was hitting line drives instead of popping up.

"Roy, there's no such thing as a level swing. I know that all of your coaches have probably told you to 'swing level,' and you'll have a better chance of hitting the ball. That's a bunch of baloney."

He'd quickly demonstrate his advice and prove to us he was right. Constantly innovating, one day he would show up with a tennis racket and tell me, "Swinging that like a bat will help build your shoulders, arms, and wrists—all of which are essential to hitting." The next day, he'd have me stand at the plate and literally throw the bat after each swing. Now, for anyone who knows baseball, you're taught at a very young age not to do this for safety purposes. This man, with his fat cigar wedged in his mouth, was telling me to throw the bat, and to throw it harder with each swing!

"Roy, this is what I want you to do at the plate. I know it's awkward, but all great hitters literally throw the bat at the ball. This is an essential concept if you're to be a great hitter."

We'd also spend hours doing "soft toss," which is a popular drill used everywhere today. As today, the batter stands facing a chain-link fence or backstop, and someone else lines up at a 90-degree angle around 10 feet away. Kenny would toss me tennis balls in this manner so that I could learn to hit the high pitch for power. The drill is also useful in teaching hitters how to adjust to different speeds and breaking pitches. Although this seems simple, at the time, Kenny would only introduce these drills to the prospects in which he was most interested.

≈ ≈ ≈

Although Kenny wasn't the type to talk about his personal life, I would get him to open up occasionally and talk about his past. I learned that he was in the service during WWII, and luckily escaped combat because he was asked to play for the Army baseball team with other pros. He'd often tell me that he thought every young man would benefit from the training and discipline he learned there.

Kenny was born in Los Angeles in 1920, and he was his parents' only child. He never really knew his father, who died when Kenny was just seven years old. As a child, he spent most of his time at the ball fields, learning baseball from the older kids—which led to his contract with the Browns at the tender age of 15. Since I was without a father, I thought that Kenny could understand my situation better than most. In one sense, Kenny was much more than a legendary scout to me. He was becoming a surrogate father figure.

Most people weren't fortunate enough to know Kenny's lighter side. He had a great sense of humor—especially after a few drinks. We used to call him "The Monk," because that's what he looked like in uniform—he wore it like a robe, and his stocky stature lent itself to the nickname. Of course, he didn't mind at all, and I think he actually enjoyed the handle. Perhaps he thought that it could've been worse; or maybe he thought the name fit. He probably believed that God had put him here to teach the world how to hit. To Kenny, baseball was truly a religious experience, and he spent more Sundays on the diamond than he ever did in a church pew.

To many people in the baseball world, Kenny was the best at teaching hitting, and I can remember many major leaguers asking Kenny to help them. In today's language, he'd be called a "hitting guru," and he was always on stage when it came to hitting. I think even my mom was tired of hearing his constant conversations on hitting, but that was what interested Kenny. If you met him, it wouldn't take you long to understand that.

Around 1965, Kenny and Tommy Lasorda were invited to come to Japan and represent the Dodgers by one of the Japanese Professional Baseball teams. The primary purpose was to watch, evaluate, and teach the professional ball players in Japan. At the time, no one in America had any clue about many talented Japanese players. Today, all that has changed. Who knows? It may have all begun with Kenny.

Upon their return, Kenny was invited to return the following year and coach a season there. Although honored, he thought that going back to Japan could only hurt his career at home. However, after lengthy deliberation and the surprising encouragement from both his Dodgers and his family, he agreed to another year in Japan. His family even visited him during their summer vacation. Yet, when Kenny returned to the Dodgers, he found that things had changed drastically. His scouting territory had been reassigned, leaving him with only half the area he had previously enjoyed. Since a scout earns his salary based on successful signings, Kenny's paycheck would be cut considerably. After much soul searching, Kenny finally decided to leave the Dodgers, following many former L.A. executives and coaches to the new opportunities waiting in Anaheim with the California Angels. That franchise named Kenny their batting coach and gave him scouting duties as well. Ironically, they hold "Kenny Myers Day" each year to recognize his contributions to the sport.

꩜ ꩜ ꩜

After meeting Kenny Myers, my life switched to a much faster pace and a more adult lifestyle. Since I was now "the man of the house," I thought I was getting the best education, and I had no complaints. We'd discuss many facets of life and lifestyle, from women to nightlife. Some of his stances, I saw later in life, were more adult-oriented and may not have always been the best of influences. For example, Kenny was no teetotaler. He enjoyed his booze and would often take my mom and me to many of his end-of-the-day hangouts. I think she enjoyed it much more than I did. He introduced her to L.A.'s social scene. Kenny would work with me after school, then he'd invite my mom and me to join him for dinner, and the evening would turn out to be quite late.

Initially, my mother would be concerned since most of these late nights were also school nights, but she seemed fine with everything as long as I got my work done. I think she somewhat agreed with me that this was part of my education as a professional ballplayer as well. I'm sure that she was curious about the lifestyle of such a man anyway. In many of these places, scouts and former ballplayers would meet to discuss the current state of the game and "the good old days." To meet and hear the opinions of some of the great players—and see what they were really like—was quite a trip for a 15-year-old boy.

Kenny knew that my father was not involved in my life. He'd often make it a point to take my mother to dinner and treat her to social evenings. She'd often say, "He is always a perfect gentleman." When he came by to see me or he'd take me to work out, he'd attempt to include my mom whenever possible. Some people would comment openly about Kenny "using" my mom to get to me. At the time, I didn't see it that way at all. I truly thought he was trying to help us. Mom had a variety of jobs, and none of them paid well. Kenny knew we were short on money, so it wouldn't surprise me if he occasionally gave her a few dollars to make ends meet. Of course, I don't know if this ever happened for sure. If so, I'm sure that he told her, "Don't worry about the money. . . . Someday Roy will be playing for the Dodgers, and you'll be able to pay me back."

As I consider the circumstances today, I have no doubt that Kenny used my mom to influence me, but he wasn't alone. Many scouts were trying to impress her. Kenny was just the best of the bunch. One could also say that I used Kenny even though I was only 15 when we met. In life and in business, people use other people all the time. I'm not saying that it's right—but it's done, and it's part of life.

After the Dodgers signed me, Kenny spent very little time with my mom, and I know that she was hurt by that. She was aware that Kenny was married and had a family, and I never thought it'd be right to judge her. Nor was it my business to explore how far their relationship truly went.

≈ ≈ ≈

Kenny expected success. He didn't hand out compliments. If I hit well, he wouldn't say a word. My impression was, no matter what I did, it would never be quite good enough. Today, as a father, I want the best for my boys. I'm sure they sometimes feel that the standards I've imposed are impossible to meet. Lord knows that no one's perfect. I want them to strive for perfection, but I also need to support them when they meet obstacles or failure. I never received that kind of support from Kenny, and perhaps it's that sentiment that only comes from someone's true father.

Until his death, Kenny was designing, patenting, and marketing a variety of hitting methods and devices. He'd spend hours studying films and photos of great hitters, searching for the perfect swing. I vividly remember many late nights, as the bar was preparing to close for the evening, that Kenny would have the remaining patrons and employees organized with makeshift bats in their hands. Every one of them swung the perfect swing—the game-winning homer in the bottom of the ninth inning of Game 7 in the World Series. Then, everyone would stagger home, and that night they'd dream that they could be a baseball hero just as easily. Kenny probably thought that was the perfect way to end the night.

Kenny passed away in 1972 at the age of 52. He died from cancer, and I lost a good friend; baseball lost a legend; and the world was a better place while he was here. Only today am I realizing the impact that he had on my life. I see Kenny's legacy in hitting methods used today, and as long as there is a bat, ball, and a game called baseball, his influence will be present.

Only today am I realizing the impact that Kenny Myers had on my life.

5
Signing a Major League Baseball Contract

Only two months before my graduation from Garden Grove High School, our baseball team was winding down, and I was enjoying my best season—two no-hitters, several one-hitters, and a .400 batting average at the plate. My baseball coach, Mike Sgobba, had done an outstanding job, and he'd later go on to the college ranks, enjoying more success that ultimately would land him a position as a pro scout. That year, I was his best player, and the league placed me on their All-League Team, recognizing me as their Player of the Year.

Major League Baseball was busy developing its draft system, but it hadn't been introduced formally. Mike, like many other coaches, scouts, and teammates, thought I'd sign a large bonus contract with a major league team—many of which were speaking to my mother regularly. I remember one scout in particular, Joe Stevenson of the Red Sox, went out of his way to do something very kind for me that I'll never forget.

In March of '61, Joe personally invited five or six high school prospects to meet him at La Palma Park in Anaheim for a "special workout." Not long after we took the field, all anxiously wondering what was so "special" about that day, none appeared but Ted Williams! Without a doubt, we were in awe. I was realizing the baseball-card dreams of my youth in Illinois. Here was the man my grandpa had called "one of the greatest hitters of all time," lamenting that the Cubs couldn't get him on their squad. I remember telling Joe that I probably wouldn't wash my hand for a week or two after Ted shook it. Williams personified perfection when it came to hitting a baseball. In my mind, no one did it better—even today. I aspired to become him, and I knew he could only help me realize my dream.

Williams had only been retired for a year when I met him, and he was taking his time to help us to improve our game in the little town of Anaheim, California. After 19 years with the Boston Red Sox, he left a void in the game he loved. There's no doubt that he would've been able to play even more seasons had it not been for his service in WWII and the Korean War. Williams was a navy pilot in both wars. He was astronaut John Glenn's wingman.

One story reported from their time together involves a mission in Korea. Williams's plane had been hit by enemy fire, but he didn't eject because he thought that by doing so he'd lose his legs. Glenn recalled how fast Williams got out of and away from that plane once he touched down, and later commented, "At that moment, he was the fastest man in the major leagues." To me, Ted Williams truly represented the best of America and a member of mankind's highest class.

Joe invited us all to meet him so that Ted could give us tips on hitting, but the day didn't go exactly as planned. Each of the players took turns at the plate as Williams watched, mixing some helpful suggestions with constructive criticism. When I got to the plate, though, he didn't say a word.

"My God. . . ." I thought. "What am I doing wrong?"

I made solid contact and hit several home runs, but I didn't hit everything out of the park. His silence started to disappoint me, and Joe seemed to notice. After I was through hitting, he called me over.

"Roy, I don't want you to be discouraged that Ted didn't say anything to you," Joe said. "He told me, 'Whatever this kid is doing, tell him to keep doing it.'"

I later learned that I'd impressed Williams, and he thought that I definitely had the ability to play at the major-league level. When that "special workout" ended, Joe invited us all to his home to enjoy a barbecue and another unique opportunity to spend time with Ted.

"The worst thing that a batting coach can do to a hitter is change *anything* when he is hitting," Williams told us. "Only when a guy is in a slump should you make any suggestions or changes, and each of you were all hitting the ball well today. I don't think any of you were slumping, so just keep swinging, and you'll get your hits."

I'll never forget that day or the advice Ted imparted. He had confirmed what I believed in my heart—that I possessed the necessary ability to play at his level. I will always remember the kindness and consideration that Ted showed me that day. Many years later, our paths would cross once more, and again, he would offer me his kindness and support under completely different circumstances.

A round the same time, the term "bonus babies" started to appear in baseball's vernacular. Unlike today, and because there was no draft, highly sought players were offered bonuses just for signing a contract. Most of these bonuses ran four to five figures, with a few in the six-figure range. In 1958, Frank Howard reportedly signed out of Ohio State with the Dodgers for $100,000. In today's terms, that would be multimillion dollars.

Kenny Myers obviously wished to sign me to a Dodger contract, and I wanted to play for them. The day of the signing, no agents were involved—just Kenny, my mother, and me. So on that warm April evening in 1961, Kenny sat down with us and presented me with the original contract. Since I was still a minor, my mother had to sign for approval. Jokingly, I looked to Kenny and said, "I think I'd like to look this agreement over. I may want some time to think about it."

Suddenly, the tension, previously hidden by the occasion itself, became barometrically tangible.

Kenny looked at me squarely and sternly said, "If you don't sign this contract right now, you'll *never* play for the Dodgers. . . ."

Roy's high school graduation on June 16, 1961. From left: Roy's sister, Pat; Roy's mother, Molly; Roy; and Kenny Myers, the Dodger scout who signed Roy.
From the Roy Gleason Collection

To Kenny, this was very serious business. His demeanor was visibly different from the moment he entered our house that night. I noticed that he was even more nervous as he pulled out the contract and laid it in front of me.

Today I wonder how that night would've transpired if my father were present. Neither Mom nor I had any experience in contract negotiation, and although the moment fulfilled a dream, the business aspects were quite solemn. Signing that contract made me the property of the Los Angeles Dodgers, and they could do what they wished with my career and me.

I quickly assured Kenny that I was only joking. I told him that he should know that the Dodgers were the only team I wanted to join. He anxiously watched as I became a Dodger with one quick stroke of his pen.

As for the contract itself, the Dodgers had postdated the terms since I was a minor at the time. I'm not a lawyer, but I always felt that this was a violation of MLB rules—possibly even illegal. Perhaps that was the reason Kenny seemed nervous. Was he looking out for my interests, the Dodgers' interests, or his own? He insisted my mother also sign the agreement, right? Perhaps this protected the Dodgers from liability should the underage issue arise. By baseball's rules, the contract was signed two months before I was legally able to do so. However, the contract provided a bonus for my mother as my "agent," and Kenny explained, "Since you're the parent of record, this is just a small token of the Dodgers' appreciation for your efforts."

I have to laugh about that—even today.

I knew that other teams were interested in signing me, but I truly loved the Dodgers. They were, after all, my hometown team. Kenny had invested a ton of time into me, and I felt that I owed him for that investment. That night, however, I saw a completely different side of him—a no-nonsense, strictly business attitude and an uncharacteristic nervousness I had never witnessed.

As my graduation approached, scouts besieged my mother with phone calls, and she would just tell them, "Roy will have to decide for himself." She never let on that the deal was already final. On graduation day, scouts surrounded my house. Rosy Gilhousen—a scout for the Angels, who were owned by my boyhood hero, Gene Autry—was letting me know how badly he wanted to sign me. He thought I'd sign with whoever offered the most money. The Angels offered me $100,000—the highest by far—but he was unaware of my previous arrangement with the Dodgers. The Dodgers—never to let a publicity opportunity pass—quickly released photos of my contract (not the original) signing at the Fullerton home of Al Campanis. In fact, after my graduation, Kenny drove my mother and me straight to Campanis's home, leaving all those scouts waiting in my front yard.

After graduation, June 16, 1961, at Al Campanis's home, Roy signs his major league contract for a reported $100,000. From left: Al Campanis (L.A. Dodgers scouting director), Kenny Myers, Roy, and his mother, Molly.
From the Roy Gleason Collection

S everal things bother me about that time as I recall those events. The Dodgers obviously acted dishonestly when they signed a minor to a postdated contact. I know that the Dodgers weren't the only team doing so, though, and no one objected. After all, I wanted to play for the Dodgers, and I wanted to repay Kenny for his investment. Still, I believe what they did was wrong, but it's all "water under the bridge," as they say. Other aspects bothered me far worse.

First, the Dodgers publicly proclaimed that I had signed for a $100,000 bonus. I'm still not sure why they did this. I only received a bonus of $55,000, which included the $5,000 paid to my mother for acting as my "agent." Perhaps they didn't want other clubs to think that an American League expansion team had outbid them. To me, it's wrong to publicize lies. Those falsities placed me in an uncomfortable position. Each time I was asked about the contract, I was instructed to tell people, "I got what I wanted." In my case, the truth hasn't been published until now.

Secondly, and perhaps most disturbing, is what I learned years later. I discovered old check stubs showing that the Dodgers had financed my mother's divorce from my father. The divorce occurred a year before I signed, but it seemed clear as I sifted through the stubs that the Dodgers were thinking strictly business from day one. They were removing potential obstacles before a contract had been drafted. The check stubs covered my mother's flight and travel expenses and the divorce attorney's fees. Obviously, my father could have made things difficult for the Dodgers later, and they needed my mother to be single for them to move forward.

As one looks at the process in hindsight, the course of events paints a very different picture. First, the Dodgers developed our trust in Kenny Myers, who wooed my mother with a lifestyle she'd never experienced. Secondly, they removed my father from the picture altogether, giving the Dodgers the ability to control the circumstances. That allowed them to sign me for far less than other teams were prepared to offer. The playing field was never fair, and the Dodgers benefited from its skew.

Truly, I mention all of this because I'm afraid the same may happen to prospects today. I hope that future athletes and their parents will be better prepared than I was—than my mother was. They should demand honesty. Obviously, we're talking about two completely different sports—Major League Baseball circa 1961 as opposed to 2005. With free agency, super-agents, and sports attorneys, the shoe may finally be on the other foot. I guess what goes around comes around.

I have to admit: That summer was one I'd dreamed about for years. My contract stipulated that my bonus would be paid in five installments of $10,000, and Kenny arranged $5,000 for my mother for acting as my agent. What does an 18-year-old boy do with that kind of money? Does he or his mother seek financial advice, or invest in stocks or business opportunities?

Come on. . . . You know what he does. He buys a new car.

Kenny suggested that I buy a new 1961 Chevy, and he took me to see Fletcher Jones in Pasadena. He helped me wheel the transaction, and I ended up dropping $3,600 cash on the car. Before I'd even signed with the Dodgers, they bought me a 1950 Chevy for $200, and when it broke down, they got me a 1953 Chevy to use. They even set me up with a credit account at the local Union 76 station so I'd always have gas. Union 76 sponsored the Dodgers' radio and television broadcasts, so it probably worked out as a barter and trade—not that I ever questioned it. Some may say that the $0.23 gallon of gas easily could be covered by the $50,000 the Dodgers saved on my contract. At the time, I thought it was the best deal on the planet.

The car, a fire-engine red '61 Chevy, was a chick magnet—and at 18 years old, what else is there in a young man's life (when he's not playing baseball, that is)?

Upon leaving the dealership, Kenny said, "Call me when you get home and let me know what your mom thinks of the car."

On the drive home the car began to smoke just as I was exiting the freeway. I frantically thought, "What kind of deal did Kenny work out for me? A brand new car isn't supposed to smoke itself off the freeway! What the hell am I going to do?"

After leaving my brand new car on the off-ramp, I walked to the nearest gas station and called Kenny to tell him what happened.

"Christ, what were you doing? How fast were you going?"

"I swear, Kenny, I wasn't speeding. What kind of lemon did they sell me?"

We both calmed down, and he said he'd be there as soon as possible. Forty-five minutes later, Kenny showed up with Mickey Hartling, one of my high school buddies, next to him in the front seat. Naturally, they were discussing the art of hitting—Kenny was going to sign Mickey as

Dodger Rookies of 1961. *Courtesy of the Los Angeles Dodgers. All rights reserved.*

a catcher. After deciding that we'd tow the car back to the dealer, Kenny removed a steel chain from his trunk, hooked it up to the car, and told me to put the car in neutral and steer it behind him.

Mickey can confirm what happened next. . . . Kenny's giant 1960 Chevy was in front of my car, and we had this chain hooked up to my shiny, new 1961 Chevy Impala. We were sitting on the right side of the road—at an intersection. As the light turned green, I could see that Kenny and Mickey were jabbering away—about hitting, no doubt. Anyway, he put the pedal to the metal and took off like a rocket. The chain's slack quickly tightened, whirling Kenny into the dash, his famous cigar bouncing around the dashboard in the wake of its ashes. From behind, I could see Kenny's hands and arms flailing wildly, learning later that he was trying to keep himself from catching on fire. Mickey was holding his neck, trying not to laugh.

"What the hell did you do?" He yelled as he jumped out of the car.

"I didn't do anything except follow your damned instructions," I yelled back.

He later admitted that he may have forgotten I was behind him. That was Kenny, though—no matter what he was doing, his mind was always on the "perfect swing." I'm surprised he didn't have more accidents. As for the car, we found that the dealership had forgotten something as well—they neglected to put oil in the car after I'd purchased it.

~ ~ ~

Although the summer of 1961 was one of the most important of my life, I'm often amused at those memories that remain the clearest.

"The Goatmaster"—the name still makes me smile. Kenny gave that name to Jim Gilbert, a good friend, and fellow ball-player on our '61 Dodger Rookie team. Kenny called all of the players "goats" and since Jim was a few years older, he hoped Jim would keep us in line. The problem was that Jim was the biggest kid and party animal on the team. He did more to lead us astray and get us into trouble than keep us in line. Even today—over 40 years later—the Goatmaster and I still keep in touch and laugh about the great time we had.

One Saturday evening in July, I had a couple of my friends in my car—Johnny Vanelli and Dennis Hartling, Mickey's younger brother. We'd all graduated together, and we were out that night to have a good time. A very attractive girl had invited us to her party in Newport Beach. We all knew that we'd be heading in different directions soon, so we wanted to put our future on hold for one evening and really enjoy the present. On our way to the party, we stopped by a liquor store in Newport Beach and picked up some booze. Since I was tall and had gone to several bars with Kenny, I managed to get a fake ID, and I had no problem securing our beverages.

As we pulled away from the store, however, the local police stopped us. Knowing that we were in deep trouble, Johnny told me to give him my fake ID, which I immediately did. Since the window was down, I figured that he'd "dispatched of the evidence." The officers asked us to stand outside the car so that they could search the vehicle, where they found the liquor and its receipt. When we produced our identification and they knew that we were underage, they questioned us about how we were able to purchase the alcohol.

"Where is the fake ID, boys?"

Some of the officers had spoken with the store clerk, who informed them that one of us had an adult ID. Yet, without evidence (the ID itself), they could do nothing. They searched us thoroughly. They searched the car several times. The scoured the area around the car and the route from the liquor store to its current point.

Finally, they took all of us to jail, where they continued their intense investigation. One would think, from their obsession with this, that we'd murdered a family. We were scared, of course, but no one said a word. After hours of detention, they finally let us go. Once outside the police station, I couldn't contain myself any longer.

"Johnny, what the hell did you do with my fake ID?"

Smiling, Johnny pointed to his mouth. Once across the street, he showed us his inky tongue, and we put together the crime—he'd stuffed the card into his mouth with his gum. We still laugh about the hours those officers spent looking for that ID. If they simply would've asked Johnny to open his mouth, they would've had a pretty good clue.

Another humorous story included Johnny and Junior Gilliam. I was going to practice with some of the Dodgers, and since Johnny was a good high school ballplayer, I invited him to join me. After arriving and warming up, we started to shag fly balls in the outfield. Junior Gilliam was hitting them to us, and Johnny was unbelievable, making diving catches, not missing a thing. Junior was so impressed that after the workout he asked him where he was playing.

Smiling, Johnny said, "Adamo's."

Junior said, "What league is that?"

Johnny and I both laughed.

"What's so funny?" asked Junior

"Adamo's isn't a baseball league or team; it's a little bar in Orange County where Johnny is an entertainer," I told him.

Johnny would later become an entertainer, inventor, and business entrepreneur. Through the years, we've managed to stay in touch despite life's obstacles.

≈ ≈ ≈

By summer's end, I was eager to see what the future had in store for me as I prepared for the winter instructional league in Arizona—my first taste of pro ball. The carefree days of high school and playing for fun were over, now that I had the financial responsibility of supporting my mother and sisters. Kenny's change in demeanor that balmy April night truly foreshadowed the change I would have to accept as part of my new, adult life. The Dodgers, my family, my friends, scouts, coaches, and other players all shared the highest of expectations, and I weighed that against the thought that, for the first time, I'd be playing with and against the best players in the world. My "special workout" with Ted Williams helped bolster my confidence, but nonetheless, the pressure was mounting.

Kenny made sure that I was in top shape before heading to Arizona in October. Only four months out of high school, my life in Orange County now seemed very far away. Arizona was a wonderful place to play baseball. The playing fields and facilities we played on were outstanding. I couldn't help remembering, as a 11-year-old driving with my family from LaGrange, Illinois, to Long Beach, California, saying to myself that no one would ever want to play baseball here. Yet, in just seven short years, I'd completely changed my mind about the desert.

In Arizona, I noticed, for the first time, how profoundly affected young women were by athletes. Of course, we all know about DiMaggio and Marilyn Monroe. I like to refer to it as, "The Power of the Game." That power makes successful athletes into celebrities to the media and fans—and makes them the ideal date (or mate) for many young women. I was never without a date throughout high school, and my time with the Dodger Rookies only enhanced that fact. However, when I began playing in the instructional league around other major leaguers, I really witnessed "the power" at work. Young ladies besieged us after each game, hoping for a chance to meet, greet, or leave with whomever exited that clubhouse door—including married players, coaches, or managers. The allure of the professional athlete has increased exponentially throughout the years, and it takes a special person to be able to handle that without self-destructing. Many times, I was left mimicking Flip Wilson, the comedian, saying, "The devil made me do it." I finally witnessed the "unlimited opportunities" my grandpa had mentioned years earlier. At least I was staying in shape. . . .

On the field, I played well, hitting over .300 against some good major league pitching and remained strong defensively. Before we played games, however, we actually went to school—learning the fundamentals of baseball. Sliding more effectively, situation play, run-downs, and all the offensive and defensive aspects of the game became my classes. You'd be surprised how many players were unfamiliar with many of the basics. I had been blessed with great coaches, so I had a head start on most of the instruction. Yet I did pick up some important lessons. The Dodgers had their own teaching methods, and I doubt if any of that has changed to this day. That's not to say the game hasn't changed—it's far different offensively, and there's far more platooning than when I played.

As the instructional league tied up its season, I was very eager to begin my first spring training in Vero Beach, Florida. I knew I had the ability to play in the majors, and I wanted to be ready when the opportunity came knocking. Little did I know that opportunity was much closer to the door than I expected.

6
First Spring Training

I still remember the excitement that I felt the morning of that Saturday in February 1962. I rarely have difficulty sleeping, but the nights leading to that morning, I barely slept at all. My dream was about to come true—I was heading to spring training. I'd besieged Kenny Myers with all kinds of questions as the day approached:

"How long is the flight? What should I take? What do I do when I get there?"

My greatest fear was missing that flight—juvenile jitters, caused by the fact that I'd be away from my friends and family for the first time. Although I was confident that I could face any major league test, I was looking for reassurances, and Kenny, along with my family, was there to provide them.

"Dodger tradition is that for spring training, for the major league players, always begins in the last week of February," I remember Kenny reminding me. "Since you've signed a contract, you'll be flying there with the veterans from LAX."

As I boarded the plane, I tried to calm my nerves amidst all the anxiety over what was to come—what was a dream come true.

≋ ≋ ≋

The overpowering aroma of orange blossoms that I first smelled as I stepped off the plane in Florida still lingers in my mind today. Although I'd grown up in Orange County, California, I'd never smelled anything as sweet. As soon as you arrived in "Dodgertown"— Vero Beach—you saw that the Dodgers had a first-class operation (one that still stands to this day). At that time, in the early 1960s, the facility was part of a vacated naval base, so the clubhouses were remodeled barracks. The major league clubhouse, which was much nicer than the minor league facility, was modified to include all the comforts at home. We each were assigned a room that we'd share with another player, maybe two. The training facility was impeccably maintained, consisting of many acres of playing fields and Holman Field—where the Dodgers play their preseason exhibition games. As I looked around the spring training site for the first time, with the beautiful Florida weather as my backdrop, I couldn't help feeling that I'd made it into heaven.

Of course, the initial reaction was enhanced once I made it into the locker room and noticed the names above the lockers: Don Drysdale, Sandy Koufax, Johnny Podres, Junior Gilliam, Maury Wills, and many more. Each of those superstars was in his prime in those years, and many of them were still my heroes—although Duke Snider and Gil Hodges were gone from the previous year's squad.

Another of my heroes was Jackie Robinson. He retired from baseball in 1956 after 10 seasons with the Brooklyn Dodgers. Just one month earlier—on January 23, 1962—he was inducted into Baseball's Hall of Fame in Cooperstown. Many said that Jackie left the game of baseball on his own terms. He opted to retire when the Dodgers traded him to the New York Giants for pitcher Dick Littlefield and $35,000. When I signed and played with the Dodgers, Robinson was the one player I really wanted to meet. I regret never having had that opportunity.

≈ ≈ ≈

The most troubling notion I had prior to spring training involved a medical procedure that the Dodgers insisted I have completed. They learned that I still had my tonsils, and Kenny informed me that I had to have them removed before I could play.

"Kenny, I've never had a problem with them—I've never had tonsillitis," I recall telling him.

"Since you are now a Dodger, and the Dodgers have a substantial investment in you, they don't want to take the chance that you'd miss any games due to a tonsil problem. Since the operation is simple and routine, they feel that you should do it right away."

At the end of September of '61, I had my tonsils removed since I wasn't playing ball. Since I was no longer a child, the recuperation period was twice as long, and since I wasn't playing ball, I hated every moment of it.

I learned right then that, although I was 18, my contract was a double-edged sword. I was no longer a person—I was a commodity, property that the Dodgers owned and could assign as they pleased without my consent. The loss of healthy tonsils made clear who was truly in charge of my future, and I was no longer in full control.

≈ ≈ ≈

Media swirled around Major League Baseball in 1962, seeing the addition of four new expansion teams, which brought the league total to 20. In the American League, the Minnesota Twins and Los Angeles Angels, which would later become the California Angels, brought the count to ten teams. The National League welcomed the Houston Colt .45s, who changed their name to the Astros in 1965; and the New York Mets, who brought a team back to compete with the Yankees for fans. Of course, these clubs started a watershed of personnel changes throughout the league, and created quite a stir amongst players at spring training and throughout the '62 season.

Of course, for some reason, those headlines had to compete with my $100,000 bonus (although it was only $55,000). Even after the signing, the press had continued to follow me. Of course, the Dodgers were quick to label me as their highest paid high school bonus baby. Some sports writers were even waiting at the airport for me when we arrived, and that attention persisted throughout spring training.

Normally shy, I really don't enjoy being in the spotlight. I felt, at that point, I really hadn't proven myself—so why were they asking me so many questions? I tried to be polite and accommodating, which probably resulted in some very silly interviews.

I recall one reporter asked, "How did it feel putting on your major league uniform for the first time, and what number did you get?"

"Well, I've been fortunate enough to wear a real Dodger uniform when I played with the Rookies in high school. There is something truly magical about getting your new and 'official' Dodger uniform and putting it on for the first time in spring training," I told him. "To me, words just can't adequately describe how it feels."

Speaking of fortunate, I was assigned number 36—formerly worn by Don Newcombe, one of the greatest Dodger pitchers to wear the uniform. Don was an All-Star, and I was very proud to wear his number. I told myself that I'd do whatever possible to distinguish that number and myself in the years ahead.

One event outstands all the media attention that I received in that first spring training, although I didn't think it was very important at the time. Still, I wonder how much it truly affected my career with the Dodgers. I like to refer to it as the famous (or infamous) "bat-wrestling event."

Apparently, Walter Alston, the Dodger manager, would challenge any of his players to "bat wrestle" with him during the first week of spring training, inviting the media to watch. Bat wrestling involved two people holding the same bat parallel to the ground as they faced each other. Each participant then twisted the bat forward until the one with superior forearm and wrist strength would prevail, causing the other to relinquish his grip as he fell to the ground.

Alston, or "Smokey," as many called him due to his chain-smoking, was beginning his eighth season as the Dodgers' manager. He'd already won three pennants and two World Series, although he'd only batted once in the major leagues—a strikeout on September 27, 1936, as a member of the Cardinals. That may have been one reason why I never heard him speak of his major league experience. He proved that you don't have to be a great ballplayer to become a great manager. Even average ballplayers can still become good managers, but Alston had taken that a step further, and he'd become a great manager. The Hall of Fame has honored him as such.

In 1962, Alston was 51 years young and in great physical shape, of which he was very proud. His competitive nature propelled him to prove to the younger players that he could still muster the ability to show them a thing or two. The bat-wrestling event was a way for him to exhibit these abilities, and it made great copy for the media.

Of course, Walt was not only the reigning champion—he'd been champion every year that he'd managed the Dodgers. I'm still not sure if he or the media invented this little circus, but they both seemed to love it. The event was held outside the clubhouse so everyone could gather to see the wizened manager put his horses to the test.

By the way, Kenny had failed to mention anything of this, but I vividly remember some of the Dodgers reluctantly challenging their boss. With a groan and a cheer from the audience, the graying manager soon dispatched of each challenger amidst the strobe of flashbulbs. Walt was not only strong, he was six foot two and easily met most of his challengers eye to eye.

Some real excitement brewed as six-foot-seven, 255-pound Frank Howard finally accepted Alston's challenge. I even heard someone yell, "Smokey's met his match now!"

Frank made his major-league debut in 1958 but didn't come into his own until 1960. In 1961, he hit .296 with a .517 slugging percentage. He signed with the Dodgers out of Ohio State for a reported sum of

$107,000—perhaps a college graduate earned that entire amount, but after what happened to me, I couldn't be sure. Nevertheless, that was his business. Frank was known for his strength and power, hitting many "tape-measure" shots (home runs over 400 feet). He was named an All-Star many times as a Washington Senator and finished his career with 382 homers.

Frank was only 25 in 1962, definitely in his prime physically. As he strode to meet the manager on the bat-wrestling battlefield, I remember thinking to myself, "Alston doesn't stand a chance. He's twice Frank's age and can't be nearly as strong."

Although Frank was four inches taller, they seemed to line up eye to eye. After smiling to each other, Smokey held out the bat to Frank. A coach yelled, "Go!" The men were off, and for a few seconds, it appeared that the old man had met his match. You could feel the tension as both men struggled for victory, and the reporters were cheering. Finally, with what must've been a second wind, Walt prevailed as the young giant released his grip. Cheers rose from the audience. Walt's expression made it obvious—his competitive thirst satisfied but not yet quenched, he was looking for another opponent to defeat.

Suddenly, I felt nervous as Walt's eyes met mine, and with a smile, he invited me to challenge him as well. As a rookie bursting with enthusiasm, I jumped at the chance to prove myself—although two conflicting thoughts were stirring: I was eager to accept the challenge because I wanted to prove that I belonged there. However, I didn't want to be embarrassed or cause anyone else the same. Nonetheless, I was honored to be included, and I confidently approached the old man.

There seemed to be a ton of excitement hanging in the air, and adrenaline was pumping through my 18-year-old body. Walt shook my hand and smiled, extending the bat with his other hand. I noticed that his hand was more like an iron vice than a 50-year-old palm as he shook mine. Seconds later, both of our hands were on the bat. Once this occurred, Walt—who was all smiles before—suddenly grew solemn, his cold blue eyes conveying a serious and competitive spirit. I suddenly

Roy "bat wrestles" with Walter Alston during 1962 spring training in Vero Beach, Florida. *Courtesy of the Los Angeles Dodgers. All rights reserved.*

felt like I was in a Clint Eastwood western, staring down the bad guy on a deserted Main Street.

Someone yelled, "Go!" We began to twist as hard as each of us could. Although he was strong, my hands were larger, and my grip was tighter. As we continued, I noticed a small bead of sweat trickling down his cheek, which—as I widened my focus—I noticed was bright red. Sweat instantly poured from my head as well, and I felt like my cheeks were on fire as I twisted the bat with all my strength while holding my breath. After what seemed like an eternity, Walt's one hand gave way, then the other, and I was left standing there with the bat in my hands. He never dropped to a knee, so we were left there, looking at each other, but I had the bat. A loud cheer erupted, and the flashbulbs popped.

I distinctly recall the look on Walt's face. He was incensed, storming off to his office without any word to the media, the players, or me. Most of the players were smiling, but some were quiet, and as I wondered why no one was happy for me, it hit me: by winning a stupid bat-wrestling contest against the manager, could I have blown my chance with the Dodgers? Had I publicly embarrassed him? The press could post that photo nationwide!

Some of the players later joked with me:

"Roy, your career's over, pal. . . ."

"You'll be playing in the Rookie League for 15 years!"

Not one of the players ever confessed that they'd let Walt win, but I began to suspect that was the case. I was definitely not as strong as Frank Howard, so why didn't he—or anyone else for that matter—beat Walt? No one had let me in on that secret or the joke at hand. Was that why they were laughing? Could it be that they were laughing "at" me? Was this my initiation? Whatever it was, I was in danger of losing my manager's support, and that scared the hell out of me.

A short while later, I asked several of the regulars if I should apologize to Walt. Most of them said the same things.

"That'll probably make matters worse. . . ."

"The less you say about it, the better it'll be. He'll probably forget about it in a few days. . . ."

I was a little worried about "probably."

"Just go out and play your best. If you're knocking balls out of the park, it will impress Walt more. Besides, he's too big a man to hold that against you."

Fortunately, when the local papers printed the picture of Walt and I with the bat, the caption noted that we ". . . battled to a draw." I was hoping that avoidance of embarrassment would help Walt to forgive and forget.

After spring training that year, however, Walt never challenged anyone else to bat wrestle.

❧ ❧ ❧

I wasn't surprised that I was assigned to the minors—it was my first year of professional baseball. I wanted the chance to have a great season and redeem myself in Walt's eyes. The Dodgers sent me to play for the Reno Silver Sox of the California League—a "C-division" minor league team. When I received that news, I was told that the Dodgers didn't want to break me in "too fast," and they felt that Reno was the perfect place for me to develop the confidence I'd need to succeed at the highest level.

The Silver Sox were managed by Roy Smalley, who played 11 seasons in the National League—five of them for my grandpa's beloved Chicago Cubs. I remember my grandpa saying, "He's a heck of a good shortstop, but he's not the greatest hitter." Since Roy played with the Cubs, I had followed his career growing up in LaGrange. Although we'd never met, I felt that I knew him. I now played for a man whose baseball card I had collected nine years earlier.

Roy and I hit it off from the start. During the season, he helped me to improve my defensive skills. As far as hitting, he'd tell me, "Roy, you have all the tools to be a great hitter. Learn to be patient, and you'll get your share of hits."

That season—largely due to Roy's tutelage—I won the Gold-Glove award for my outfield play. However, I was disappointed with my offensive performance. Although I hit 22 home runs and walked over 100 times, I batted just .254 and may have led the league in strikeouts. My frustration was evident, and Roy told me, "Don't get down on yourself—just keep swinging. Sooner or later, you'll be making contact more consistently. Great home run hitters often strike out. The year that Babe Ruth hit 60 home runs, he also led the league in strikeouts."

Thinking back today, I realize that the essence of hitting is as much psychological as it is physical. I realize what Ted Williams and all the great hitters had—an intense mental focus that is so sharp, doubt never enters the mind. They knew they would make contact with the ball.

The Reno Silver Sox in 1962. *From the Roy Gleason Collection*

Unfortunately, in 1962, I had no concept of this focus, and I thought that my problem was purely physical. That misconception resulted positively, spurning me to work even harder during the off-season so I would get my shot. Roy told me at the end of the season, "Gleason, for your first year you did just fine." I knew that "just fine" wouldn't get me to the majors, and I reached a new low in confidence. Compounding that assessment with the bat-wrestling debacle made me feel even worse. I could only pray that, by the start of the next season, all up to that point would be distant memories.

≈ ≈ ≈

As I focused on baseball, the world continued to turn in 1962. John Glenn was orbiting the earth in Friendship 7. U.S. Army advisers were helping the South Vietnamese Army relocate South Vietnamese peasants for their safety. America's involvement was increasing, and ironically, I paid very little attention. A Supreme Court decision banning prayer in schools sparked protest nationwide. The

Cuban Missile Crisis caused everyone who dismissed world politics to pay close attention, and it definitely opened my eyes to the world at-large. I remember feeling fatalistically secure. I didn't think that both leaders wanted to die or see their loved ones perish, so no one was going to push the button. If they do, we're all goners, so why worry? I was more concerned with what I could control—reducing strikeouts, hitting the curveball, playing in the major leagues. If we didn't blow ourselves up in the months ahead, I'd be heading to my second spring training soon, and the new season brought new opportunities to realize my dream.

As fate would have it, that's exactly what happened.

7

The Majors Came Calling

I n late August 1963, I was coming off a great season with the class-B Salem (Oregon) minor-league team when I received the telegram from the Dodgers. As I read the short correspondence, my sweaty hands began to tremble. My prayers were answered, and I'd been given the opportunity of a lifetime. That telegram represented an exclusive invitation to attend a special party and experience a dream come true. I had a very difficult time containing myself, immediately bear-hugging my manager, Stan Wasiak, who had just handed me the telegram.

From day one of that season, Stan and I hit it off. During the season, he worked very hard with me on every aspect of my game, and I credit much of my success that season to Stan. He knew baseball inside and out, though he'd never played in the majors. A feisty ex-marine, Stan also spent some time as a professional boxer—he had the broken nose and cauliflower ears to prove it. Everyone knew not to give him any flak. Of all that Stan taught me that season, patience was the most important thing.

"Roy, most ballplayers fail to realize that patience is a fundamental in both life and baseball," Stan told me. "Take the pitcher who likes to work fast. Suddenly, he gets into trouble, so he tries to work faster and ends up with disastrous results. What he needs to learn is patience: slow down, take some time, make the batter wait, and gain focus. It

Roy scores from second for Salem in 1963. *From the Roy Gleason Collection*

makes all the difference in the world. The same idea applies to hitting. I see most kids go up to the plate, and before the pitcher has even thrown a pitch, the kid is up there taking countless practice swings. Watch some of your greatest hitters—when they go to the plate, they might take one or two practice swings, but that's it. Then they focus, zero in on the zone and the pitch. You need to work on this, and I guarantee you'll hit better."

Stan was right—I listened, and I hit better. The Dodgers must've thought Stan was as good as I did. They gave him an award for most minor league games managed, and he is recognized throughout baseball for his contributions to the game.

I'm sure that Stan put in a good word for me with the Dodgers administration, and they respected his opinion. He told me that I'd be playing in the majors many times during the season.

"Roy, you have the ability, and sooner or later, you'll get your chance," he'd say in his managerial tone. "For now, work hard so you won't disappoint either of us."

Work hard I did. I caught fire in the second half of the '63 season, leading the team and league in hitting, home runs, and RBIs. Over the last six weeks, I hit .370 and slammed 16 homers, and at times, I felt there wasn't a pitcher alive who could get me out. My confidence was at an all-time high, and I knew I could help the Dodgers—if they'd only give me the chance.

Considering this was only the second year that I'd played professional baseball, I was blessed to get the chance in Los Angeles. Ability is nothing without opportunity. Many great ballplayers have gone without that chance. Perhaps it's luck. Perhaps it's timing. All I know is, whenever opportunity knocks, you need to be ready. I was ready, but I knew that I had to raise my abilities to a completely new level.

Although I enjoyed a great season in '63 statistically, a couple of incidents stick out much more in my mind. The first is the night that the lights "went out." During the middle of a night home game, a power failure left us all standing in the dark. Yet, that wasn't even the funny part. Here's what happened: we were in the field, and I was playing right. The batter hit a sharp grounder to our third baseman, Rollie Petronovich, who knocked it down. As he threw the ball to first, the lights lost power. The place was pitch black for almost 10 minutes. When the lights came back, fans saw our first baseman, Dick McLaughlin, spread-eagled on the ground with a baseball in his mouth. We didn't know if he was dead or alive, but everyone knew he'd be missing some teeth. Our infielders ran over to his motionless body, and as they stood over him, he opened his eyes with a grin, revealing his practical joke.

Unfortunately, the other event that I remember was more of bump in my road than a joke. I sustained a painful injury one night as I slid into home. Though I was safe, I broke my left hand. Minus a few minor muscle strains, I'd never been injured before in pro ball, and it sent me into a deep depression. I was playing the best baseball of my life at the time, but the hand sidelined me for three weeks. Since I'd not yet learned that the Dodgers were promoting me, those three weeks were about three lifetimes long. I couldn't stand watching everyone play from the dugout.

"As soon as I get the okay from the doc," Stan kept telling me, "I'll have you back in the lineup. The worst thing we could do now is to bring you back too soon. You could delay the healing or run the risk of ending your career." The Dodgers sent me back to L.A. to see Dr. Kerlan, who treated my injury. Then I returned to the team.

Although he meant the best, all I kept thinking to myself was, "Why did this happen to me? Why now? Maybe I should just pack it up and head home."

Stan really made the difference during that tough time for me. He could see that I was discouraged, and he could've told me to deal with it—then gone about his own business. Stan knew that I was a large investment as far as the Dodgers were concerned, and he wasn't going to let that investment go down the drain.

During my second week on the disabled list, Stan decided to put me to work, intrinsically knowing what medicine I needed.

"Gleason," he said, "I want you to get off your duff and help this team by coaching third base. Having a broken hand doesn't mean you have to sit there and mope all the time. I want you out there supporting your team vocally and morally."

Suddenly, each game took on a new meaning, and I learned the significance of coaching baserunners. A base coach is the eyes and ears of each runner, and it's his job to keep them tuned in to the game situation. A coaching mistake will cost the game, and that made me feel like I was important and useful again. Stan's lesson quickly taught me that even negative experiences can produce positive results.

Once my injury finally healed, I rejoined the lineup and completed a spectacular season. Fate had tested me, and I developed the patience to pass the quiz. As a result, I was blossoming into the player that the Dodgers had hoped I'd become.

In September of 1963, the Dodgers were in the thick of a pennant race with the Cardinals. According to Stan and Kenny Myers, the Dodgers felt that I could bolster their outfield. They liked my abilities as a switch-hitter, my golden glove, my strong arm, and my speed. Some coaches remembered a situation from the instructional league in Arizona the previous year. Lou Brock was on third as I caught a fly ball—he tagged, and I threw. As he looked up in his final steps, he found the catcher waiting on him, ball in hand. Even though Lou Brock had an incredible career, setting the stolen base record (only to be broken later by Rickey Henderson), if you asked him about that day, I bet he'd remember that play. The Dodgers knew that my strong arm could cut down the opposition's options with men on base or if a hitter thought about stretching a gap single into a double. A strong arm could make all the difference in a pennant race—all I needed was the opportunity to flash mine.

Thus, that telegram was like Christmas in September. I called my family to share the news, and they were ecstatic.

"My prayers have been answered, Roy," my mother said with joy. "We'll all be there to cheer you on!"

"Be sure to call everyone in LaGrange, including Grandpa Bill," I said.

"Oh, I will. . . . I'm sure they'll be very excited! They'll probably want to know when you'll be coming to Chicago to play the Cubs! The whole family will be in the stands."

"Whom will they be rooting for?" I asked with a smile.

"You know they're die-hard Cubs fans, but when you're there, you know who they'll be rooting for, Roy," I remember her telling me.

I began to imagine Grandpa Bill and Uncles Art and Fred sitting in Wrigley Field when the Dodgers came to town, and I could hear them saying, "Damn those Cubs! Why didn't they sign Roy? Why did they let those 'bums' get him?"

≈ ≈ ≈

My flight from Salem to Los Angeles was delayed due to weather, which unsettled me. I was stuck on the tarmac trying to repeat the words that Stan had taught me: "be patient, be patient, be patient."

"It's better to be stuck on the tarmac than to take off and crash," I thought—which was a hell of a thought.

"Wouldn't that be my luck," my mind continued. "I'm finally called up to the majors, and en route, the plane crashes."

After that thought, I was glad we were stuck there. The weather cleared, I said some prayers, and we landed safely in L.A. hours later. Kenny met me at the airport, filling my ears with what I needed to hear.

"I've been following your progress, Roy," he said. "I'm glad the front office finally agreed with me about you. You deserve this shot."

During our ride, Kenny mentioned Joe Moeller, Dick Nen, Phil Ortega, and Derrell Griffith—guys who I'd played with both on the Dodger Rookies and Instructional League who also had been called up.

"When will Jimmy Campanis get his shot?" I asked Kenny.

"You probably have as good of an idea as I do. How's he been doing at Salem?"

"He's having a good year."

"It's got to be difficult for Al. . . ." Al Campanis was Jimmy's father and an executive with the Dodgers. "Jimmy's a good ballplayer on his own, though, and that's why I signed him. Still, he'd probably get a better shot if he were with another team."

I'd known Jimmy since high school because we competed against each other. He was a catcher at Fullerton High School, and I remember many exciting games when I was pitching for Garden Grove. Jimmy had good size and a strong arm, and I could see why Kenny liked him and signed him in 1962. Jimmy was my roommate at Salem, and he was as excited as I was when I told him I was being called up.

As it turned out, Jimmy did get his big break with the Dodgers during the 1966 season. He played six years in the major leagues, and today he is still involved with baseball, doing public-relations work for the Dodgers.

By knowing both Kenny and Jimmy, I did get to know Jimmy's dad, Al. I think I was only 15 when Kenny first introduced us. I learned that Al played with the Brooklyn Dodgers in 1943, playing in seven games, but his career was cut short due to a serious injury. His love and knowledge of the game took him from the playing field to the front office. His career of nearly 40 years began as a scout and later as the Dodgers' director of player personnel.

Regretfully, Al's career was shortened when he agreed to do an interview on ABC's *Nightline* with Ted Koppel involving the baseball career of Jackie Robinson. Al was asked at the last minute to pinch-hit for another Dodger spokesperson. Al's response to the question of why no blacks managed in the majors was considered a racial slur. After the show and a storm of media attention, the Dodgers asked him to resign.

I did see that interview, and I thought Al's comments were blown all out of context. He was never a bigot or a racist. Both Al and Jackie were roommates. They shared a longtime friendship that included a love of baseball and a belief in a country without racial barriers. Al did not deserve the treatment he received from the media, the Dodgers, or anyone else. Luckily, I had the opportunity to tell him that before he passed away in 1998. I hope that history will be kind to him—he was a good man, and there wasn't a racist bone in his body.

Kenny rarely got excited about anything, unless you wanted to argue about hitting. On the ride from the airport, he was calm as usual, but he stressed the importance of timing and felt that this was my best chance to make my mark.

"For Christ's sake, you're young; you've only been out of high school for two years. To have this shot at your age is great. Just go out there and show them what you can do. The Dodgers like to reward their top minor league players with chances to play at the end of the season, and that could result in a permanent position. They'd like to see their investment start paying off. Besides, there's another reason why they called you up."

"What's that?" I asked as I gazed out the window.

"They want to protect you from the expansion draft," he answered. "Many other teams may have an interest in your abilities, and this will protect you from going elsewhere."

For the first time, I truly considered myself a Dodger.

"I won't disappoint you, Kenny. All I need is a chance."

Although I was outwardly confident, I was beginning to feel the stress. My family was depending on me to do well. They'd experienced financial difficulties since my father left us; that is, until I signed my bonus contract. I again understood that I was the sole supporter of my mother and youngest sister, and that pressure was more than I'd ever experienced. Nonetheless, my mother and sisters were elated to have me home. I didn't realize it at the time, but they were feeling the pressure, too.

⁓ ⁓ ⁓

Again, my opportunities were set against a backdrop of social unrest in America; and again, like most Americans, I was oblivious to how the "times were a-changing." The South Vietnamese conflict continued to escalate as military leaders assassinated the premier and his brother. More American lives were being lost, and our involvement increased, contrary to promises from government officials. In 1963, though, I certainly never thought that conflict would involve me.

Much of the news in '63 concerned the issue of racial segregation. Martin Luther King was speaking to 200,000 people at the Washington Monument as I was shagging flies in Salem. His "I Have a Dream" speech became the rallying cry that changed this country over the years. For some, the changes have been significant, while for others, they have been much less so, slow in coming, and long overdue.

On another note, I was receiving congratulatory calls from many of my old teammates—from high school to the minors. Even the Goatmaster, Jim Gilbert, imparted some fatherly encouragement.

Perhaps it was because I was the first of our group to be called up, but even today, we get together to reminisce—they still tell me that they remember where they were when I made my major league debut. I assured each of them that it'd only be a matter of time until they joined me, and I'd be calling to congratulate them. Each time, as I hung up the phone, I imagined how fun it would be to be playing with all of them again. We all shared the same dream, and my promotion signaled that they'd get their chance soon.

Now all I needed was the opportunity to play—being called up offers no guarantee. The Dodgers were in the middle of a heated pennant race with St. Louis, and Kenny had informed me that my chances would be few and far between.

At least I was there, and maybe, just maybe, I would get my shot. I told everyone I'd make the most of it—and I think I did.

8
Playing in the Major Leagues

Recalling the flight from Salem to Los Angeles still seems like a surreal dream, and times come when I wonder if it was real at all.

The plane was packed to the brim, and I remember thinking, as my luck would have it, we'd never get there. Trying to dismiss the thought, I closed my eyes and tried to nap throughout the wait and flight, if we ever got off the ground. That's when everything became somewhat disturbing.

Two distinct voices woke me from the slumber, and as I looked up, I noticed a couple of gargantuan stature approaching in the aisle. The husband, who easily weighed 350 pounds, and wife, an easy 300 pounds herself, were bickering as they sat directly in front of me. I childishly thought, "With all this weight, the plane will never get off the ground."

As the pilot monotonously announced that we'd be delayed until the weather cleared, I noticed through the crack between their seats that the wife was digging through her purse nervously. The next thing I knew, she had found her rosary beads, which she held close to her face as she rocked back and forth, praying aloud.

Confused, or maybe curious if anyone else was watching the same show, I turned to the guy sitting in the aisle seat next to me. He was whiter than a sheet, and his eyes were closed so that veins were popping out of his head. Suddenly, he jumped from his seat and shouted, "I've got to get off the plane now! I've seen this! I had a dream last night that we're going to crash into the sea, and everyone's going to die!"

I didn't panic right away, but that changed as the guy contiuned to scream to the flight attendant, "We have to get off this plane!"

At that very moment, the engines fired, and we began taxiing down the runway. Other passengers were becoming visibly nervous. The rotund lady in front of me was stretching her seat's hinges to their limits as she rocked more violently while praying even louder. The guy next to me returned to his seat, and, with his teeth clenched and a white-knuckle grasp on the armrest, he continued to wail, "We're going to crash! We're going to crash!" as the plane gained speed.

The wheels of the aircraft finally left the ground, and as we ascended the flight attendant was yelling, "Everyone please be calm! We'll be landing in Los Angeles in a short while!"

I have to admit—I started hyperventilating as the plane gained speed on that runway, and panic ensued all around me. Once we were in the air, everything became more tranquil. The guy next to me began to relax, and he loosened his grip, allowing proper coloring to return to his face and hands, and finally opened his eyes.

"I'm sure everything will be fine, buddy," I whispered to him. Trying to take his mind off the imminent catastrophe in his mind, I tried to break the ice. "So, do you have family in L.A.?"

After a deep breath, he said, "I'm going there on business. We live just outside of Salem."

After convincing herself to put the rosary away, the portly woman in front of me turned to her placid husband and began chatting. His body language made it clear that he'd been through this before.

As we landed, everyone let out a sigh of relief, as either fate or the Good Lord had invited us all to get on with our lives.

Roy's first "glamor" shot with The Dodgers.

K enny Myers took me to the stadium clubhouse the next morning and showed me where to put my things. It was then that I received my official Dodger uniform (number 36) and my own locker. Standing in that empty room, I glanced over the names of men who were both heroes and legends to me. At 20 years old, I was sharing a locker room with baseball gods, and although I'd shared space with them during the previous two spring trainings, this was totally different. I think now that I was too young or immature to appreciate that moment as much as I do today.

Pete Reiser, one of the Dodgers' base coaches, found me there and thought it'd be a good time to go over the signs with me. I have to admit while he was teaching me the signs, I think that the surreal flight, lack of sleep, and general anxiety I was feeling severely affected my retention. I nodded my head as he spoke, but in reality, the words were going in one ear and out the other.

"Hopefully," I thought, "if I'm called upon, I'll have the chance to go over them again."

I tried to show everyone that I was calm as I dressed for the game, but right beside me—pulling up his blue socks—was Dodgers base-stealing legend Maury Wills. Don Drysdale and Sandy Koufax were right across the room, laughing and joking with each other.

Each of the players and coaches made it a point to stop by my locker to deliver welcoming and encouraging words—all but one. Walter Alston, the manager, said absolutely nothing to me. Although I was still worried that he held the bat-wrestling fiasco against me, I tried to reassure myself that he was busy, and his thoughts were consumed by the pennant race. Perhaps I just wanted to think that he was merely quiet, but to me the truth is, he wasn't a very pleasant person. I remembered the contempt in his eyes that day in Florida, and millions of concerns immediately popped into my head.

"Is he still mad? I mean that was over a year ago. They wouldn't have called me up if he didn't like me, would they?"

Roy's first Dodger uniform after being called up in 1963.

I took a deep breath and smiled. "I'm here, in the majors, and I can't worry about the past. I can't worry about whether Walt likes me or not. If he gives me the chance, I'll just go out and do the best I can. If I can play well and help the team win, then he'll know that my only goal was to help him win the pennant."

As I ventured onto the field for the first time, butterflies were dogfighting in my stomach. The stadium was empty, but I imagined it full of people cheering for the Dodgers—cheering for me. Soon they'd be there, and I prayed that I'd have the chance to impress them. After warming up, we took batting practice, and with each swing that I drove the ball, my confidence and calm returned a little. As some swings resulted in balls hit well beyond the fences, I knew that I belonged there.

Some of the pitchers began shouting at me as I continued to stroke the ball.

"Save that for the game, rookie!"

"Nobody's going to throw you that pitch in the game!"

"What kind of bat are you using?"

"Unbutton your shirt and take a real swing!"

I smiled and hit the next pitch over the fence in left-center. Someone quickly yelled, "Next!" and I grabbed my glove and headed for the outfield, invigorated by my performance. I knew Walt and the other coaches were watching.

As usual, Walt said nothing as I jogged by him. Fans were beginning to filter into the stands, filling a third of the stadium. Some of the children down by the dugout were yelling for autographs.

"Hey! Mister!"

I turned to see a young black boy behind me in the outfield stands.

"Hey, mister! I got one of your home runs. . . . Would you sign it for me?" he asked.

"Sure," I said as I walked to where he stood.

With a huge smile, the boy asked, "So who are you?"

"My name is Roy Gleason," I said with a grin.

A bit disappointed, he handed me the ball, probably upset that I was not Frank Howard.

"What's your name, son?"

"Anthony, sir. . . . I'm going to play for the Dodgers someday."

"What position do you play?"

"Outfield mostly, but I pitch some, too."

Handing him the ball, I said, "I was just where you are a few years ago, so keep playing, and maybe someday, we'll be playing together."

Taking the ball from my hand, he said, "I hope so." With a wide smile, he ran to join his friends.

My first autograph—as I would hope most ballplayers think—was very special to me. I wonder today if that young man, Anthony, ever did make it into professional baseball. I never did learn his last name, so if you're out there, Anthony, I'd love to hear from you and know how life has treated you. And if you have that baseball, I'd love to see it!

꙰ ꙰ ꙰

Reporters were loitering around major players by this time, but I drew no attention, which was fine with me. The stadium continued to fill, and the buzz became more intense by the second. A mystique fills the air during this unique period before the ballgame— one that goes through distinct stages. It all begins with the true baseball fan—the one who shows up an hour before game time and watches the team warm up, take batting practice. He turns on his transistor radio to catch Vin Scully's pregame analysis. He's in the stands no matter how the Dodgers perform, and he believes that Dodger Stadium is his second home.

Around 30 minutes before game time, that buzz rises into a random but orchestral arrangement of entering spectators. It's a beautiful noise, a swelling of emotion much like an overture. Their heightened concentration seems to attune your senses to a higher level. The lights are brighter, the infield dirt is redder, the grass is greener, and even the stadium seats look like streetlights. Odors start to imprint memories in your mind: the satisfying aroma of freshly cut grass, the sweet, initial hint of cigar smoke, steaming popcorn, and roasted peanuts all complement the moment's tapestry.

Finally, we come to the moments just before the game begins, and all the action is still around the field, but not on it. Reporters scramble for interviews. The pitchers pop the catchers' mitts in the bullpen. Organ music lays the soundtrack. Field crews finish their last-minute preparations as the sun sets behind the outfield wall. As the sky slowly dims, one can see the moon just over the mountains. The managers meet at home plate as the public address announcer welcomes the fans and presents the starting lineups. A celebrity is introduced to throw out the first pitch, and then a well-known vocalist delivers the national anthem. Then the home team takes the field, and it's "Play ball!"

I prized all of this, and I learned that this process results in a "crowd personality." Although I don't possess a degree in social science or a doctorate in psychology, I've watched crowds' responses over the years, and their combined energy creates a personality of its own. If the game is going well for the home crowd, their positive energy can propel their team even further. If the opposite is happening, the crowd's silence speaks volumes.

〜 〜 〜

I recall this because, on this particular evening, I studied the crowd intensely from the dugout as the game progressed. The Dodgers were battling the Cardinals for the pennant, and the fans were riveted by every pitch, every swing. The game was critical, and here I was, right in the middle of it all. If I earned my chance and didn't perform perfectly, I knew that the team, definitely the manager, and now the fans would never forgive me. In the back of my mind, I began to hope that I wouldn't be called upon—at least that way, I couldn't screw up.

"What good would that do?" I asked myself. "That's contrary to everything you've striven to be."

Through nine innings, I sat on the bench—the game tied, we headed to the 10th. For nine innings, I didn't even receive a glance from Walter Alston, and although the situation was crucial, I still had the feeling that he didn't like me. I kept repeating Jackie Robinson's words in my mind, "let your play be your voice. . . ."

Fate reared its head in the bottom of the 10th. Alston sent Bill "Moose" Skowron to pinch-hit for our pitcher, Claude Osteen. As I watched him inform Moose, he abruptly turned to me.

"Gleason, if Skowron gets on, you'll run for him."

The game took on a whole new meaning with Walt's gruff command. For the first time, I might have the chance to play. Skowron walked up to the plate as the announcer informed the fans of the switch. My energy switched, too—from "on hold" to "on high" in a single second. I stood and stretched to alleviate some of the nervousness.

As fate would have it, Skowron sent the first pitch up the middle for a single, and my adrenaline boiled over as I was announced to 50,000 fans. I tried to channel that adrenaline into my body, using the crowd's energy as my own. I knew that if I screwed up that energy would drain from me as quickly as the crowd would grow silent. My feet felt like feathers as the first-base coach came up to me and explained the situation.

"Listen, Gleason, there's nobody out. Remember to watch Pete for the signs."

In a panic, I glanced to Pete Reiser, who was busy flashing signs across the diamond—the same signs that he tried to teach me before the game. There was only one problem. . . . I didn't remember any of them. I think that the first-base coach must've read my expression, because he stepped toward me and yelled, "For Christ's sake, don't get picked off, either!" Attempting to decipher Pete's signs, I developed the most sickening pain in my stomach.

"Was that the steal sign or the bunt sign? Wait . . . isn't that 'hit and run'?"

I couldn't figure it out to save my life. To complicate things even further, Bobby Aspromonte was playing third for Houston that day. He used to date my sister's friend, so he's giving me a hard time between pitches, yelling across the field and trying to distract me.

"Roy!" the first-base coach yelled, trying to reestablish my focus. "We're down one here, and you represent the tying run, kid. Be ready!"

Luckily, Junior Gilliam, who singled to right field after taking a couple pitches, deciphered the signs for me. I danced over his sharp grounder, and my adrenaline carried me all the way to a safe slide into third base. The crowd erupted, rising to its feet, and yelled collectively as Wally Moon came to the plate. On the first pitch, he sent a deep drive into the gap, and I can still hear Pete yelling, "Make sure you stay on the bag! Don't leave the bag until I tell you!" Everything changed to slow motion as I waited an eternity for that ball to fall. The crowd's cheers muffled the sound of the catch, and I glanced to Pete, who was screaming, "Go! Go! Go!," but I didn't hear anything, just read his lips. Off like a shot, I crossed the plate with the throw still en route, and the crowd went crazy. Like 100,000 volts of electricity, the crowd's cheer leaves a pulsation that's undeniable. My run had tied the game, which we later won.

Although that was my only appearance of the game, I felt like I'd contributed to a major win, and more opportunities were waiting around the corner. All my teammates congratulated me, making me feel like part of the unit. Pete Reiser came up to me after the game, and said, "Roy, you did great out there tonight, and you're really going to help the team. Stay focused and do your best. You're young, and you have a bright future ahead of you." As far as baseball moments go, that was the highest I'd ever known.

After showering, I dressed quickly and walked back to the dugout alone, climbing the steps to the field so that I could savor the moment. The vacant stadium—which I think is the most beautiful in America— made me feel at ease. The butterflies in my stomach were gone for good, chased away by a successful day. I had reached the elusive gate and passed through it—this was the big time, the big show, the ultimate.

≈ ≈ ≈

A few games later, I'd finally reached another pinnacle. After pinch-running in several games—I scored three times—I was finally called upon to bat.

As the final days of the season approached, the Dodgers captured the pennant from St. Louis, and the final games made no difference in the standings. On the faces of coaches, players, and fans, the relief was obvious. Walt could play anyone now, and he'd already exhausted most of his bench. Rather than let the pitcher risk injury with a late plate appearance in an unimportant game, Walt uttered the magic words.

"Gleason, I want you to pinch-hit for the pitcher."

Behind by six runs, we all had the feeling that the game was already finished. On his way to coach third, Pete Reiser pulled me aside and said, "Roy, you're leading off. This is your first major league at-bat, so forget that we're getting killed and go out there and show them what you've got!" I fumbled around the dugout, trying to find my bat.

"Rookie, you need to get out there now," someone yelled.

"I'm going . . . I just need to find my bat!" I yelled to everyone in general. Finding it hiding in a corner, I grabbed it quickly and ran to the on-deck circle. I took some practice swings as I watched the Phillies' pitcher, second-year southpaw Dennis Bennett, pop the catcher's mitt with his warmups. Bennett was around six foot five, and on that day he looked like a giant on the mound, but I wasn't intimidated. The last practice pitch thrown, the catcher flung the ball to second, and the infielders tossed it around the horn.

"NOW BATTING FOR LOS ANGELES, NUMBER 36, ROY GLEASON. . . ."

Again, my adrenaline soared off the charts. Since I was a switch-hitter, I decided to bat from the right side so that I could see the ball better. Bennett nodded to the catcher and delivered the first pitch, which looked like a changeup, low and inside.

"BALL!" shouted the umpire.

I turned to the catcher and said, "Why is he throwing a changeup to a pinch hitter?"

"That was his fastball, rookie," the catcher snapped back.

I took a couple practice swings as Bennett examined the signs. Without shaking him off, he delivered another "fastball" right at the knees on the inside corner. I watched the ball, which looked like a basketball at that point, right off the barrel of my bat, driving it down the left-field line. Out of the box in a flash, I sprinted around first and slid safely into second—although no throw was made. The crowd was roaring, and as I stood, I realized that I'd just hit a double in my first major league at-bat! I couldn't wait to get up again—I had enough energy pumping through me to hit the next pitch five miles!

Now Walt would see that I could hit as well as run. The next batter, Dick Tracewski, hit a line drive up the middle, and I scored standing up, bringing the crowd to its feet.

When the game ended, I realized that my at-bat was an amazing moment in my young life. It signaled the accomplishment of a goal— the manifestation of a dream. The season was over, and I just hoped that Walt would give me more opportunities during the next season.

Team	G	AB	R	H	2B	3B	HR	RBI	BB	IBB	SO	SH	SF	HBP	GIDP	AVG	OBP	SLG
1963 (Dodgers)	8	1	3	1	1	0	0	0	0	0	0	0	0	0	0	1.000	1.000	2.000

Unfortunately, I hadn't played enough games to be eligible to join the Dodgers in the World Series. Thus, I wasn't a part of the Dodgers' historic four-game sweep of the Yankees in the '63 Series. I tried to focus on the year to come and another opportunity to prove to all of Los Angeles that I was a true player—one who was there to stay.

≈ ≈ ≈

I was in the clubhouse when it happened—in the Arizona Instructional League. The day was gorgeous, so I decided to head to the ballpark a bit earlier than normal. The '63 season had just ended, and I was eager to refine my skills for '64. Bill Parlier, our switch-hitting bonus baby from Lakewood, California, rushed into the clubhouse.

"Did you guys hear?"

"Hear what?"

"Roy, the president just got shot. . . ." he muttered solemnly.

"That's not funny, Bill," I said.

"I'm not joking, Roy. Turn on the television if you don't believe me!"

Other players began filtering into the clubhouse with the same expression, so we turned on the television to confirm that President Kennedy had been assassinated in Dallas. Every person in the clubhouse that day had welled eyes.

For the first time, the world was placing my life into perspective. A month earlier, the world was my oyster. Kennedy's death made everyone, even a young man having the time of his life, stop and think about the world in which he lived. Civil rights issues were tearing the country apart from the inside. In South Vietnam, people were dying in droves, and even Buddhist monks were setting themselves on fire to protest the conflict. Now our president was dead, and for the first time in my life, I found myself asking, "Why?"

No pandemonium ensued—just an inert sadness that stopped everyone and everything. Our game was postponed immediately, and the following Monday was declared a national day of mourning. I suddenly realized that, no matter who we were or where we are, our lives could end in a single moment. For me, that day signaled the end of innocence. I realized that safety was a mirage, and I no longer felt invincible. I understood that I'd been sheltered from reality for most of my life, and danger is truly present in each of our lives.

That understanding would carry me through even tougher, blind-siding times—times that were racing opportunity to my door.

My thoughts in 1963 were captured by Charles Dickens's classic, *A Tale of Two Cities*, in which the opening sentence reads, "It was the best of times, it was the worst of times." Playing perfectly in the majors was "the best of times" for me, but for his family and his nation, the president's death brought "the worst of times."

9

Hollywood Highlights

Being a Major League Baseball player certainly has its perks—especially in the 1960s. Playing ball in Los Angeles afforded me many opportunities to meet celebrities of the stage and screen. As today, the old adage, "It's not what you know but who you know," was very important then. A baseball player could earn the same American-celebrity status some enjoy today—the flavor of the day, so to speak. You start receiving invitations to social functions that you'd never receive—let alone hear about—without it. All of a sudden, you're on a first-name basis with decision makers in Fortune 500 companies, movie studios, television and radio stations, advertising agencies, and everyone else involved in the entertainment industry.

For most of my life, baseball was just a game. Soon after becoming an official member of the Dodgers, I understood that baseball was a part of show business—our responsibility was not limited to our physical abilities. We had to entertain as well. That included a level of obligatory interaction and appreciation of the fans. When I see the *prima donnas* of today's game, I remember that we understood that the fans paid our salaries. We were role models, because we did influence others—especially children. We may not have had to raise the children, but we represented something that they wanted to become. I know, because I was one of those children.

As I became someone who people noticed in Los Angeles, I fell into acquaintance with legendary sports photographer Frank Worth, who was also the official photographer of the Dodgers. Frank also made a good living as a still man in Hollywood. The night that I signed my contract at Al Campanis's home in Fullerton, it was Frank behind the camera.

Around that time, Frank had told me, "If you're ever interested in working in Hollywood, give me a call." Of course, I was flattered at the time, but I never gave it much thought because of my budding baseball career. After making my Dodger debut in 1963, Frank called, urging me to give the proposal another thought. Some other Dodger players filled small roles in television and films, and Frank assured me that I had "the look" that Hollywood liked. After the mention of little work for good money, I decided to give it a shot. He wanted to act as my agent, and he would call me if I got any auditions.

A few years earlier, Chuck Connors had gone from professional baseball to instant celebrity with *The Rifleman*, and to this day, he's remembered as an actor. Frank saw me similarly.

"Roy," he'd say, "you're young, six foot five, and you have what they're looking for. . . ."

Before long, I had performed a few parts in both television and film productions, and even though my first love was still baseball, Frank continued to remind me that my entertainment work would add many years to my income.

Today, I know that he was right, but acting wasn't something that I wanted to do, and one needs talent to survive in that business. Truly, I thought that the Hollywood lifestyle was superficial. Naïve as it was, I believed that people in baseball were more honest and forthright—at least the players were. Of course, I soon learned that occupations don't dictate a person's honesty—a liar is a liar whether he's a janitor or a judge.

Around Christmas of 1963, I landed a guest spot on a new television series called *Branded*, starring Chuck Connors. Before a scene, Chuck called me over to discuss the dynamics.

"Roy, do you have any experience riding horses?" he asked.

"Sure, Chuck, I know how to ride horses," I said. "I just have a little trouble steering them."

Speechless, his face did all the talking. "Is this kid serious?"

We broke into laughter and continued the shoot.

Somehow, a Hollywood writer picked up the conversation, and in his column, he used it to say that jocks weren't the sharpest tools in the shed.

I got a good laugh out of it. By the way, I rode the horse and steered him just fine.

Another television opportunity arose when Frank introduced me to the producers of *No Time for Sergeants*. I think that a book later became a play starring relatively unknown actor Andy Griffith. The play and Andy were big hits on Broadway. Hollywood executives signed Griffith to play the same part in the movie production, and it achieved significant box-office numbers. That film was then made into a television series.

The show was a sitcom about a young man, raised by his father in impoverished Appalachia and possessing little formal education. Everyone's first impression of him is that he's dumb, but in reality, he's honest, trusting, and sincere. The plot unfolds as a local draft-board officer arrives to inform the father that Uncle Sam has drafted his son. From that point, the calamity and hilarity ensue.

Frank thought that I'd be perfect for many recurring roles, so I went to the auditions. A casting director struggled to think how he'd heard of me, finally asking, "Aren't you the Dodger who can't steer horses?"

Nodding, I smiled and realized why Frank thought I'd be perfect for the part of Will Stockdale. I later learned that the leads had already been cast, but the casting director wanted me for some guest spots. Next thing I knew, they had me in an air force uniform taking publicity photos with some of the girls from the show.

Unfortunately, Hollywood offers no insurance, and the show ran just one season.

Roy Gleason (left) and Sammy Jackson talk on the set of No Time for Sergeants in 1965. From the Roy Gleason Collection

≈ ≈ ≈

As a young, single, professional baseball player who appeared in movies and television programs, I enjoyed many opportunities to meet many very attractive women. I'm not the type of person who kisses and tells because I believe in privacy, and celebrities often sacrifice that right.

Nonetheless, sometime around Halloween in 1964, Frank called to tell me that he'd arranged a blind date at a costume party located at a swanky Hollywood nightspot.

"Everyone's supposed to dress up like his or her favorite nut," he told me. "So what's your favorite nut?"

"Are you kidding me?"

"No."

He waited patiently as I thought.

"I don't know, Frank . . . cashew, I guess."

After thinking for a second, he laid down the plan. "All right, this is what I want you to do: wear a nice white shirt, taping dollar bills to your sleeves and chest. You'll be all set—a 'cash-u nut.' Trust me, you'll be a big hit."

He was right. My blind date, a stunning actress by the name of Mamie Van Doren, loved the gag, and several young ladies asked me if they could take some of my cash. My first time at a true celebrity event was a whirlwind of famous people. I met Jayne Mansfield, who did a very revealing number atop a grand piano. I also met Natalie Wood and many other beautiful ladies that night. I was like a kid in a candy store.

Although I'd been around adults my entire life, I was still very naïve about some things. While at the bar, a young man around my age sat next to me and asked, "Do you like to go to gay parties?"

Now, you have to remember: I'm the guy who said, "I can ride horses, but I have trouble steering them. . . ."

When asked if I liked "gay parties," being the 1960s, I thought he was referring to a "fun party," so I said, "Sure, I enjoy a good time."

Roy chats with the girls from *Broadside* in 1963. *From the Roy Gleason Collection*

The guy asked me for my phone number, and as I was writing it down, Frank approached.

"Roy, what are you doing?"

"I'm writing down my phone number for this guy—he wants to invite me to gay parties."

"Christ, Roy! Don't you know what 'gay' means?"

Confused, I said, "Having a good time?"

"No, Roy," Frank muttered, "it means he's a person who prefers the same sex, you schmuck. You don't prefer guys, do you?"

"Hell, no," I said as I tore up the paper.

Frank turned to the young man, who was still trying to process the turn of events. "How the hell did you get in here?"

Embarrassed, the guy looked away and quietly said, "I just crashed it."

Shortly thereafter, he was escorted out by security.

Being somewhat naïve, I was surprised and offended at the time. I realize that many different lifestyles exist, and while I don't understand the gay lifestyle, if it doesn't involve me or my family, it's really none of my business.

A few days after all of this, I received a call from Buzzie Bavasi, vice president of the Dodgers, telling me that he needed to see me immediately. On my way to Dodger Stadium, I was filing through all the potential conversations, hoping that Buzzie would say, "Roy, we've decided that you've earned a spot to play the entire season with us next year. How does that sound to you?" He sounded serious on the phone, and I couldn't think of another reason for him to call.

That's when I thought about it further and realized that Buzzie didn't sound happy. In fact, he sounded as though something was wrong.

"What the hell did I do now?" I thought.

I carried this worry into his office as his secretary led me to a seat. Buzzie sat behind his desk, puffing a long cigar. I could see that he was nervous as well, and after some small talk, he leveled with me.

"Roy, I called you here because I've been reading some things about you in the local papers, and I'm concerned about how some of it may affect the Dodger organization."

"What do you mean, Buzzie?"

He nodded, taking the cigar from his mouth as he eyed me seriously. "How was she, Roy?"

"What?"

"How was she?"

"Who is *she*, Buzzie?"

"Roy, don't give me that bullshit—I read all about it." He grabbed a newspaper and tossed it in front of me.

"What did you read in the papers?" I asked, still confused by everything.

He tapped on the paper and yelled, "It's in all the Hollywood gossip columns, Roy—YOU and MAMIE VAN DOREN!"

The beautiful Ann Marshall. *Courtesy of Ann Marshall*

I guess the day after the party, a small article had printed something like, "Who was that six-foot-five Dodger rookie seen with Mamie Van Doren at one of Hollywood's hottest costume parties?" I was both surprised and disappointed—I thought he'd be telling me about my future with the organization and instead he was asking me about a damn costume party. "Who was there? How did you get the date with Mamie? Did you drive her home? Did you sleep with her? Will you be seeing her again?"

"Sorry to disappoint you, Buzzie, but nothing happened. Yes, I drove her home, but nothing happened. I might see her again, and that's my business. You don't have to worry—I won't embarrass you or the Dodgers with my personal life."

I walked out of his office, and I think he was more disappointed that I didn't have any juicy details for him than he was concerned about the Dodgers. I learned that day that the Dodgers read the gossip columns as well, so I made sure to be more discreet about who I saw and when. My private life was going to be anything but private, and I'd worked too hard to blow my baseball career on a one-night stand with an actress.

That being said, I dated several beautiful women besides Mamie, but the most significant of those relationships developed between me and Ann Marshall, who was the daughter of famed British actor Herbert Marshall. We dated on and off for over a year, but then drifted apart.

～ ～ ～

The list of celebrities I met during this era is very special to me, and I'd like to share some of those memories with you:

DEAN MARTIN

I met Dean in the late '50s when the Dodgers were playing in the Coliseum. Kenny took me to the game and led me to the areas where many celebrities would sit. He introduced me to Dean, who was real—exactly as he was on television and in films. Dean was a huge Dodger fan, and he attended most home games. He wished me well, and I remember seeing him often during the '63 season at Dodger Stadium. He was a great entertainer, a great fan, and we all miss him.

FRANK SINATRA

Frank was special to me as well. Like Dean, he was not only one of the world's greatest entertainers, but a huge Dodger fan as well. Frank loved baseball, and I had the opportunity to meet him many times on and off the field. I saw him perform many times, including his show at the Cal Neva Lodge at Lake Tahoe. I also met him on the set of *Von Ryan's Express*. Frank Worth and I visited the set, and Mr. Sinatra invited us to his trailer. I remember that the trailer had several bedrooms at each end, and Frank joked that Mr. Sinatra surely used each of them fully. Each time I hear one of Frank's songs, I recall days when his smile seemed to make the world happy. I miss those days, and the entire world misses Frank.

JOHN WAYNE

"The Duke" was a boyhood hero of mine. I used to ride the range in my cowboy outfit, trekking through the forest preserve in LaGrange. Even today, he remains one of my heroes for many reasons. I truly believe that he led his life much like the characters that he played. He was always the good guy—in movies and in real life. We initially met on a movie set, and I'd often speak with John at charity events and social functions. Hollywood has never been the same since he rode into the sunset, and he'll never be forgotten.

NAT KING COLE

Nat often attended Dodger games, where I met him during the '63 season. We chatted in the dugout before a game, and I remember that he had a cigarette in his hand, and his voice was soft and melodic as he spoke. I was terribly sad when he died in 1965. Few realized how ill he actually was. His impact on music will last forever.

JERRY LEWIS

I first met Jerry in 1958. I was still in high school, and Kenny asked me to go to Wrigley Field in Los Angeles to pitch batting practice to the Dodgers and some major league all-stars for an annual charity event. Jerry was the only celebrity who participated. He played first base, and he was good. I think he could've played pro ball. For many years, Jerry played in that game, and I remembered that he hit well when I was pitching—much better than I expected. I later worked with him and several other Dodgers in the movie, *Which Way to the Front?* I had a small part as a German officer who takes out a machine-gun nest. Jerry also played a German officer, and in the scene we share, he pins a medal on my chest. Jerry has two personas. On screen, he's normally a clown. Off camera, he's all business, directing the action and letting everyone know who's in charge—a completely different

On the set of *Which Way to the Front?*—from left: Paul Winchell, Roy, Jerry Lewis, and Don Sutton in 1970. *From the Roy Gleason Collection*

Don Sutton takes a bite of Roy's ice cream bar on the set of *Which Way to the Front?* in 1970. *From the Roy Gleason Collection*

person. I'll never forget the times we shared together and his delicious pastrami sandwiches.

NANCY SINATRA

I met Nancy shortly after she made it big with "These Boots Are Made For Walking." She was very sweet, and she definitely had the Sinatra music gene—although she made it without hanging onto her father's coattails. She did share her father's love of the Dodgers, though, and that's how I met her. I definitely would've liked to have dated her around that time, but I believe she was married. Today, I hear that she does a radio show with her brother and sister. I doubt she'd remember me, but I wish her and her family much continued success.

AUDIE MURPHY

I met Audie long before I served in the military, but it was still an amazing honor. I was on a movie set at Universal Studios when I saw him. I remembered my parents telling us about his bravery in WWII. I believe he's the most highly decorated soldier in American history, and at the time, his deeds were legendary. That bravery and recognition led him to a very successful career in film. After what I've experienced, I have very few heroes, but Audie Murphy is certainly one of those.

≈ ≈ ≈

Looking back, I feel very old to think that many celebrities I met then have since passed away. The world lost some very special people, and the Dodgers lost some very important fans. As Frank Worth would say and Frank Sinatra would say, though, "That's life. . . ."

I was sorry to learn that Frank Worth recently passed away. He was always honest with me, and he had a way of presenting the truth without allowing you to feel rejected. That's a rare trait in Hollywood. Frank was able to make me a significant figure for 15 minutes when I was only a kid. I understand that, even today, he's a legend in many Hollywood circles.

In a recent television interview, Buzzie Bavasi revealed that a top Hollywood producer had approached him about me, saying, "When the Dodgers are through with him, let me know because I want him for the movies."

Turned out that Frank was right, but he understood that my real and only mistress would never be a Hollywood actress or fame itself, but the game of baseball continues to seduce me over 30 years later.

J ust before I was drafted, I was up for a regular part in *F-Troop*, but that opportunity was lost to the U.S. Army. Ironically, *F-Troop* was based on a fictional "Fort Courage," and when I was later stationed in Vietnam, I was stationed at a French fort nicknamed "Fort Courage."

Not long before that, I'd auditioned for a war movie, but the director told me that I was "too big" for the part. From Vietnam, I wrote that director:

"While you told me that I was 'too big' to play in your war movie," I wrote, "it seems that Uncle Sam and the U.S. Army had no problem finding a uniform big enough to fit me when sending me to Vietnam and hell."

I didn't think that I'd ever receive a response. As it turned out, I was right.

10
Back to the Minors

After the 1963 season, which ended with the Dodgers' World-Series sweep of the Yankees, I truly felt that my performance in eight games would earn me a break-out season in 1964. During those games, I played well in every area of the game, carrying a perfect one-for-one plate performance into '64. In October of '63, as the Dodgers were winning the Series, I was sent to the Instructional League in Arizona—and it was there that I got into a little trouble.

I did something stupid, which always I blame on my youth. After another long day of ball in December, we were all hoping for a break. Just a few weeks after we were all still trying to recover from the shock of Kennedy's assassination. Many of our games were canceled around that time, and we were scrambling to make them up, so many of us could've used a day off.

One Saturday night—after our seventh or eighth straight game—a few of us headed to a local bar, where I proceeded to drink a few too many. Feeling no pain, we decided to head back to the ballpark, and I figured that the field could use a good watering. We turned on the hose and sprinkler system, got a bit carried away, and left the plate area and most of the infield flooded. Seeing as we were a bit off-kilter anyway, we decided to increase our fun. Starting at third base, we sprinted into the soaked circle around home plate, sliding over the muddy puddle.

We did quite a number on that field. I'm sure we're not the only people who'd ever done this—I remember our scene playing out while watching *Bull Durham* years later. After our mischief, I ended up riding to our hotel on the fender of a teammate's car. Once there, I decided to bathe myself (I was covered in mud) in the motel's pool. An elderly lady witnessed my late-night clean up, and I'm pretty sure that she reported this to the motel manager.

To make matters worse, my watch fell from my wrist at some point during the entire escapade. Since I wear a size-15 shoe, Danny Ozark, our manager, had a pretty good idea who was involved. Forced to report the matter to the front office the following day, Danny handing me the phone, saying, "Buzzie wants to talk to you!"

"Roy, what the hell were you doing last night?" Buzzie asked.

"What do you mean?" I asked naively.

"Don't give me that bullshit—you know what I mean, damn it. You flooded the goddamned field, and now they have to cancel today's game!"

"Who said it was me?"

"They found your watch at home plate, and no one but you has a size-15 shoe print. . . ."

I was positive that my career was over. "What do you want me to do?"

"You've caused enough trouble at this point," Buzzie said. "Why don't you just come on back home?"

Although my actions were obviously immature, all of my teammates gave me a standing ovation when I came to grab my stuff from the clubhouse. Danny was pissed at first, but he suddenly broke into a huge smile, and said, "Hey, what you did was very dumb, but we all needed some time off. Forget about it, and enjoy your vacation." With that, he shook my hand and sent me home. As I headed for my car, I prayed that my actions wouldn't destroy my future with the Dodgers.

D uring the last week of February, all the contracted Dodgers leave L.A. for Vero Beach and spring training. In 1964, the Dodgers had an Electra propjet fly the entire team to Florida. Welcomed by the same sweet smell of orange blossoms, we encountered nothing like I had ever experienced. The media was out in droves, vying for exclusives with our star players—the Dodgers were world champions.

I was much more confident heading into that spring. I'd grown stronger, logged two years of minor-league ball under my belt, and even tasted, albeit briefly, a bit of the majors. I'd proven that I could hit major-league pitching, and all I needed was "the chance."

No personnel changes had been made from the championship team, and considering my limited exposure, I knew that it'd be almost impossible to break into the starting lineup. To make matters more difficult, I strained a few muscles during spring training, which negatively affected my performance. No sane manager changes a winning combination, and Alston wasn't crazy. I would've done the same thing.

Although I expected my assignment, I was still disappointed to learn that I was headed back to the minors. I learned later that most players spend an average of four years in the minors before getting a chance. Very few were as fortunate as I was. I accepted the assignment reluctantly. Occasionally, I'd asked Kenny Myers and my coaches where I stood with the organization, and they'd always tell me the same thing.

"Roy, be patient. You'll get your shot, and once you do, you'll be playing for a long time. . . ."

I remembered Ted Williams telling me, "You'll have a hell of a career in the major leagues," but I was 20 years old and very impatient. I started to wonder whether my future would include the Dodgers or another team.

～ ～ ～

My assignment took me to Albuquerque, New Mexico, which was considered Double A. The team was managed by Clay Bryant, a former Cub pitcher who finished with a career record of 32 wins and 20 losses. For the most part, we didn't hit it off well. We used to call Bryant "Tiger Eyes," because of the way he'd scowl at us. I believe that his attitude held many of his players back.

For example, if we lost or played poorly, he never helped us learn to correct our mistakes. Instead he'd prop himself atop a chest in our dressing room—that secured all of our valuables—wearing nothing but his jockstrap and say nothing at all. We'd finish showering, dress, then wait in silence until he decided to move his fat ass so we could go home. Perhaps that was his way of forcing us to consider the game instead of hitting a nightclub. Honestly, it was just immature—and hypocritical. Many evenings he'd beat us out of the clubhouse to chase the ladies. I made the mistake once of dancing with a girlfriend of his, and the next thing I know, I'm headed back to Salem.

Since I didn't like playing for Bryant, I didn't mind the change. My statistics were solid, so everyone knew that my demotion was personal. I even remember Bryant telling me, as I arrived, "You're here because the Dodgers thought you could use the playing time, and sitting on the bench up there wasn't going to help you any."

I was happy to be reunited with Stan Wasiak in Salem, and he was delighted to have me in the lineup.

"Roy, you'll be a huge help to us," he told me. "I've followed your success through the levels. Just be patient, and you'll get your chance. You'll be playing for many years."

I knew he meant every word that he said, but I started to feel like I was moving backwards. Shortly after arriving, things got worse—I pulled a groin muscle and sat for much of the season. I hadn't helped Stan at all, and I felt like my future was in a far darker cloud than ever before.

The '64 season proved disappointing for the Dodgers as well, as they finished with a losing record 13 games behind the Cardinals, who won the World Series in seven games.

The Dodger front office prepared itself for major changes, and since I was completely healed, I figured '65 would be the year for me. I strove to improve my physical prowess and shape so I could avoid any minor injuries that would impede my progress.

The events of 1964 sent our country spiraling in a completely new direction. The Beatles took the world by storm, and I had no idea that one of their songs would be so important to me a few years later in a land far away. Lyndon Johnson had stepped into Kennedy's shoes after the assassination and set forth his own agenda. In August 1964, Johnson urged Congress to grant him broad emergency powers regarding Vietnam. The North Vietnamese reportedly attacked a U.S. Navy destroyer, resulting in the Gulf of Tonkin Resolution—a motion that legitimized our continued involvement in Vietnam. I may have read about this, but I wasn't concerned since I was classified 3-A, exempt from military service.

≈ ≈ ≈

I reported to spring training in great shape thanks to Pete Reiser. I'd taken my physical abilities for granted up to that point, and I knew that I couldn't let another season—another chance—slip through the cracks. Fortunately, 1965 spring training was my best to date. Major personnel changes led me to believe a regular spot was just around the corner.

Gone was Frank Howard, who was traded to the Washington Senators after Gil Hodges took the managerial reins there. Gil also acquired Bill Skowron, Dick Nen, and Ken McMullin, also former Dodger teammates. These moves brought my play to light, but for some reason, I was assigned to the minors again.

The 1965 Dodger starting outfield originally consisted of "Sweet" Lou Johnson in left, Willie Davis in center who fractured his ankle in

Roy with the Spokane Indians in 1965. *From the Roy Gleason Collection*

May and was replaced by "Sweet" Lou Johnson, and Ron Fairly in right. Fairly moved to the outfield from first base, which Wes Parker now manned. I knew that I had a better arm than Fairly; and I was considerably faster and batted from both sides of the plate. Alston and the Dodger brass obviously disagreed. Ron had seven years of experience over me; and he batted in the high-.200 range. He also had championship experience, which was probably the deciding factor.

Instead of going back to Salem, the Dodgers sent me to Spokane, Washington, their Triple-A club in the famed Pacific Coast League. Although I was disappointed, the new manager, my good friend, Pete Reiser, quickly turned me around. As fate would have it, though, Pete suffered a serious heart attack, and he was replaced by Bill Brenzel. We were all heartbroken, and I believe that under Pete's skilled management, I would've had the season I needed to get back to the majors.

Bill Brenzel was far from Pete Reiser. Prior to becoming manager, he'd been scouting for the Dodgers—and was appointed temporary manager until a permanent manager was hired. Bill had far less major league experience, and there seemed to be a generation gap between him and the players. Perhaps my friendship with Pete hardened my opinion toward Bill. Perhaps it was that Bill not only didn't care for Kenny Myers, he thought that his ideas on hitting were ridiculous as well. Fortunately, I think for everyone, Bill was soon replaced. Unfortunately, Pete's loss affected the entire team, and our performance suffered.

Bill's replacement was none other than Duke Snider, one of the Dodgers' most famous alums. He played 16 seasons with Los Angeles, and his stellar career earned him a place in the Hall of Fame. As a kid, I used to watch him on television and then imitate him on my baseball field. I saw him play at the L.A. Coliseum as a teen and met him in the late '50s through Kenny Myers. Just one year out of baseball, he was coming to manage my team. Ecstatic, we all knew that his experience was just the jolt we needed to turn around the season.

Personally, I wondered if he remembered me. We played together during spring training in '62, and I'm sure he heard about the "$100,000 bonus." Duke was present when I bested Alston in the bat-wrestling match, so I wasn't sure whether or not he viewed me in a positive light. He was coming into a very difficult situation—assuming control of a floundering squad midway through the season. Because Duke was an outfielder and hit for power from the left side, I hoped he'd impart his knowledge, but the entire team's troubles prohibited him from individual instruction.

I loved playing for Duke, but no matter what I did at the plate, nothing was falling, and I was in a serious slump. My mind was so preoccupied with a promotion that I couldn't focus at the plate. In late April, I pulled my hamstring, and Duke had seen enough. In order to rebuild my confidence, the Dodgers sent me down to Salem after I healed. As the 1965 season came to a close, I continued to flounder, and I was finally sent down to Class-C Santa Barbara for my final games.

I had hit bottom. I was almost certain that I'd never see the majors again. My perfect performance at that level had been obscured by my lowly .250 average in one of the lowest divisions of professional baseball.

I kept asking myself, "What the hell am I doing wrong?"

I received similar answers from my managers and coaches, other players, and even friends.

"You're just trying too hard."

"You're psyching yourself out."

"You're overcoached."

I got to a point where I truly thought that I should give it all up and look into the opportunities Frank Worth was offering in Hollywood. During this soul-searching period, I found the most meaningful advice in my mother's words. She made me realize that I wasn't a quitter, and I could turn things around—that bad seasons, just like good ones, come and go.

"Roy, look at the great ballplayers. There is not one of them who has had only good seasons. No human being is perfect. You need to stop feeling sorry for yourself, work harder, and you'll have the season that you earn and deserve. That's the way life is, so accept it, and always do your best. The rest will take care of itself.

"Look at the Dodgers. They won the World Series in 1963, and you played a part. In 1964, they were near the bottom, and you had no part in that. Now they're having a great year, and you're not there. But you and I know that you have the ability; you've proved that. So, you had a bad season. . . . That doesn't mean that you'll have a poor one next year, so go out there and make your sisters and me proud of you."

I don't think that Knute Rockne could've given a better pep talk. I got off the ground and dusted myself off. I knew deep in my soul that quitting baseball would never be an option.

Roy's grandparents visit Garden Grove prior to spring training in 1966.
From the Roy Gleason Collection

∽ ∽ ∽

Although 1965 was a low for me, the Dodgers were enjoying a pinnacle year. They faced Minnesota in the Series, pitting their top-shelf pitching staff against the Twins' hefty power hitting. The Dodgers won 2-0 in Game 7, proving once again that dominating pitching and defense overcomes offensive firepower.

While Los Angeles went crazy, I had some mixed emotions. The outfield played a huge part in the Dodgers' championship, and I knew that the lineup was even harder to crack than before. I just prayed that 1966 would be the year.

≈ ≈ ≈

The end of 1965 brought my financial arrangement with the Dodgers to an end. My $55,000 bonus had expired, and my mother no longer had money to pay the mortgage. I assured my mother that I'd continue to help her, but the added pressure wasn't helping my chances. The strife permeating our country added to these tough times: riots in L.A., race issues, and the escalating conflict in Vietnam. Still, I was more concerned with the upcoming season.

After a solid showing in spring training, I was still shipped to play for Duke Snider again, this time for Tri-Cities of the Northwest League. I was a much better player than he'd seen in Spokane, leading the league in home runs and RBIs. When our regular first baseman broke his leg, Duke asked me if I'd like to move to the infield.

"Our infield would have to throw the ball into the next county to get it over your head," he told me.

The Tri-City squad in 1966. Duke Snider was the manager, and Roy led the league in six statistical categories, but was drafted the following year. Roy is pictured top center. *From the Roy Gleason Collection*

I made the transition smoothly, winning the Gold Glove and was selected to the league's all-star team. By season's end, I had regained my confidence, found a new position, and poised myself for another shot in Los Angeles.

The Dodgers succeeded as well, winning their second consecutive pennant behind their Hall-of-Fame pitching staff. Favored to win their second straight championship, they met the Baltimore Orioles in the World Series. The teams matched up even offensively, but the Dodgers' pitching staff gave the Dodgers a formidable edge.

In Los Angeles for Game 1, a sellout crowd witnessed that pitching dominance fail to shut down Frank and Brooks Robinson, and Don Drysdale was defeated by Dave McNally 5-2. In Game 2, Sandy Koufax took the mound against a 21-year-old sophomore named Jim Palmer. Although Sandy was only 30, he suffered from severe arm pain but still managed to hold the Orioles scoreless through four innings. Willie Davis committed three crucial errors in the fifth, and Sandy was replaced by Ron Perranoski. He couldn't stop the bleeding, and the Orioles prevailed 6-0. Palmer was magnificent, extending the Orioles' string of shutout innings to 18. Sadly, the game was Sandy Koufax's last of his Hall-of-Fame career. He retired a gentleman, a professional, an icon, and a legend.

Dodger fans everywhere were falling in a tailspin. Two home losses didn't reflect the dominance of the previous two seasons. I called up Kenny Myers.

"The Dodgers need me *now*."

"You're right," he told me. "But they just don't know it."

"Isn't there something you can do?" I pleaded.

"I'm afraid not, Roy."

I could tell he was just as disgusted with the way things were going.

As the Series rolled to Baltimore, nothing changed for the Dodgers. They lost Game 3 1-0, and Baltimore dominated Game 4 as well, going 33 consecutive innings without allowing a Dodger to cross the plate. The sweep sent a message to me: The Dodgers needed bats, and my '66 season was proof that I was their man.

≈ ≈ ≈

As 1966 wound down, news from Vietnam became less optimistic by the day. The term "search and destroy" was becoming a part of our everyday vocabulary, and a wave of antiwar protest was sweeping the country. Due to increased military action, the government increased its calls for young men. The country continued to struggle through civil rights conflicts, and we teetered on the fence of political change. Still, I was concerned more with my baseball career than global conflict, obsessed with the chance to be a regular starter in the major leagues.

Unfortunately, neither the Dodgers nor I could make that happen.

11

The Day My Life
Changed Forever

My chances with the Dodgers were limited, but I still felt that I had a chance to take Ron Fairly's place in right field.

"Fairly's only drawback is that he doesn't have the best wheels," Kenny pointed out. "You could play rings around him in the outfield. I can't believe they didn't bring you up when they sent Frank to Washington."

As kind as Kenny's words were, Fairly hit .288 in '66 and solidified his place in the lineup. My only other option was Wes Parker's spot at first base. However, Wes was also a consistent hitter, and I couldn't imagine Alston choosing me to replace him.

My only other choice was a trade. Kenny and I had discussed it, but he felt that the Dodgers would be foolish to trade me.

"The Dodgers would prefer to keep you in the minors than take a chance on you playing for some other team. They can protect you from the expansion draft as well."

So I was draft proof—and that's how I arrived at spring training in 1967.

⤜ ⤜ ⤜

As spring training began, news reports revealed that U.S. forces were shelling targets in North Vietnam for the first time. Although this had always been a distant notion in my mind, an explosive moment brought the war to my door.

April Fool's Day, 1967, was the day that changed my life forever. I thought the letter was a joke, but the letterhead looked official, and the message sounded official. It didn't take me long to realize that this correspondence from the Department of Defense was the real thing.

The letter, which began with "Greetings," was my official draft notice. I was finishing one of my best springs, and I was devastated. I've never considered myself a religious man, but I believe that the Good Lord has a way of delivering circumstances to our lives that test us spiritually and mentally. I kept asking God, "Why, after coming so close, am I now being asked to do this?" I didn't want to be a part of the brutality. My life was caught up in a game, but this was no game. Young men were fighting and dying in a small Asian country, or protesting the war and all it represented. I couldn't bring myself to be bothered with either—my dream was at stake.

That's not to say that I didn't care—I believed in this country, and I was willing to fight and die to preserve our freedom and way of life. But at 24, I was classified as the sole supporter of my family, supposedly exempting me from the draft. To receive a draft-board notice two weeks earlier that my classification had been changed from 3A to 1A came as a complete shock.

I immediately informed the Dodgers and asked for suggestions on how to proceed. Some other players near my age were also concerned. The Dodgers, rather than risk them being drafted, advised them to volunteer for the Army Reserves. Since I was now in the same boat, I asked the Dodger brass if I should go into the California National Guard. However, they informed me that I had little to nothing to worry about, suggesting that I'd be better off simply appealing the reclassification. They said that they didn't want me to miss any of the season, which might happen if I joined the Army Reserves. As the sole supporter of my family, the Dodgers felt that would be enough to keep me safely on board.

Listening to this advice turned out to be very foolish on my part. I didn't consider the possibility that the Dodgers knew only as much or less about my situation than I did. I'd put my entire stock in their wisdom, and I made a mistake.

The Dodgers may not have realized that Congress was calling for more troops for the war effort. I'm sure they missed the memo that Congress was busy writing a landmark $70-million defense appropriations bill, later signed by President Johnson—the largest money bill in the history of Congress. Perhaps they were unaware that Johnson had promised General William Westmoreland 47,000 additional men, so that by mid-year, over half a million soldiers would be in Vietnamese jungles.

Dodger management did suggest that I contact an attorney and my local congressman, which I did. The attorney filled out the necessary paperwork, and the congressman made a few calls to inquire about my status. Both assured me that my appeal was in the works, and that I'd just have to "wait for the system to work." Nothing happened, though, and I grew worried.

When April 1 came, less than two weeks before my 25th birthday, I received my notice of induction, listing the time and place to report. I asked the Dodgers to intercede on my behalf, but they simply dropped out of the picture.

"We are very surprised to learn this. . . ."

"We can't believe that the army's drafting *you*. . . ."

"We're sure that your appeal will come through. . . ."

I knew that I was completely alone. I learned later that some Dodger officials even said, "[The army] will probably be good for Gleason; he'll learn some real discipline."

I'm sure that the draft board felt, "As long as he can play baseball, he can go and fight with the other young man we draft daily."

I suppose I could've refused to serve for religious or political reasons, or fled to Canada as some students and protesters had. I felt that was wrong, though. If I had to go, I would go. Don't think that I was "gung ho" about going to Vietnam. Like many other young men, I was frightened and prayed that I wouldn't be sent.

Kenny told me that he was lucky during WWII. Since he was a professional ballplayer, he spent much of his time in the service playing ball. I hoped I'd be as lucky.

◆ ◆ ◆

The induction center was littered with the concerned faces of young men. Searching for a familiar face, I couldn't help thinking that misery truly does love company. Everyone was confused and nervous, and one could feel the tension in the air. We were finally ushered into a large room where a uniformed staff member announced that we were going to be sworn in. He informed us of the penalties for refusing the oath in a very serious manner.

"Does anyone object to taking the oath?" he asked the throng.

Rarely intimidated, and sensing others' displeasure, I thought that many hands would reach for the sky. I was quite surprised to find that I was the only guy with his arm raised. I couldn't believe it—didn't they know that they could die half a world away? I'd never felt so alone in my life. Everyone was staring at me, jaws agape, and then I noticed two of my buddies staring at me with big smiles.

Gary Mulleady and Bill "Wazy" Wasdyke called to me as two military induction officers escorted me out of the room. I knew Gary from high school, and we still socialized occasionally. I met Wazy through him, and we all partied together from time to time. Unfortunately, I couldn't share their levity as I was being led out of the room.

The induction staff informed me that my refusal could result in a possible $10,000 fine and up to five years in prison. Under these circumstances, they convinced me to take the oath, then work on my "hardship discharge" as sole supporter of my family and the only surviving male of my household. Still, I was determined to follow through on my appeal.

Those guys told me, "Don't worry—you'll probably be playing baseball on some base during your entire tour."

"Yeah, that'd be great," I said. "But can you guarantee that?"

⁀ ⁀ ⁀

After that point, things moved very quickly. The next thing I knew, I was on a bus to basic training at Fort Ord, which is near San Jose. An outbreak of spinal meningitis caused us to move to Fort Lewis, Washington, so we could complete the training. Although I had my attorney filing a formal protest to my reclassification, I immediately approached my commanding officers and requested further paperwork for a hardship discharge.

Because I was in good shape, basic training was fairly easy. I had trouble keeping the hours, though. In baseball, our day began long after sunrise, late in the morning—and our games were in the afternoon or evening. In the army we were waking three hours before sunrise and going until it was dark. Gary and Wazy's presence helped take the edge off as well. By June of 1967, basic training had ended, and my concerns increased.

I'd still heard nothing of my appeal. Contacting my attorney, I frantically attempted to get a grip on the situation.

"Don't the people who hear these appeals realize that the clock is ticking? I could be sent to the front and die before my paperwork crosses their desks!"

"I understand, Roy," he'd tell me. "I'm doing all I can. These things take time. Just try to be patient."

That sounded gratingly familiar. Being patient while waiting for your time to come in baseball was much easier by comparison.

Roy graduated from basic training at Fort Lewis, Washington, on June 16, 1967. Roy is in the front row, third from the left. *From the Roy Gleason Collection*

My hardship discharge application had met a similar fate. I was sure it was lost in a stack of the same, collecting dust. Periodically, I'd check on its status, but I was always told the same thing.

"The application was processed along with many others. We assure you that you'll receive immediate notification once the decision is made."

Somehow those assurances only increased my frustration. My family was flailing financially, and I didn't know how I'd be able to support them from Vietnam. Their letters continued to be positive, but I had the disturbing feeling that what they weren't saying could mean the worst.

Upon graduating from basic training, I received "expert" marks in my military occupational specialty (MOS), classified 11B10—I was now a private in Uncle Sam's infantry. The honor included a trip to Fort Polk, Louisiana, for advanced infantry training (AIT).

We all knew that Fort Polk was the last barrier between Vietnam and us. Some lucky souls were sent to Europe, but most of us knew we were going to hell, and the clock was ticking louder with each passing second. After arriving, I heard about a leadership-preparation course (LPC), and I decided to sign up for it. Hopefully, the class would buy me some time for my appeal and discharge claim to work through the system before I was shipped.

Two weeks passed, and the class was over, but I'd still heard nothing. To buy more time, I took the airborne ranger course, which lasted several weeks, then took the advanced infantry classes for eight more weeks. From basic training in June to September in Fort Polk, I kept praying. Neither came through, and finally, I received my orders—I was headed to hell.

⇒ ⇒ ⇒

Actually, some good news accompanied my activation orders as well—I received a 30-day leave. The month-long window gave me the opportunity to make another appeal regarding my reclassification and hardship status. My family and many friends sent letters to the appeals board on my behalf. You never know who your true friends are until a time of crisis, and I cannot thank those people enough. I've kept copies of those letters, and they're very dear to me. Pastor Weirsig of St. Paul's Lutheran Church in Garden Grove sent several letters. His sermons on God's love were very important to me at that time and stay with me today. I hope he realized the impact he had on my life.

Ironically, Kenny Myers never sent a letter on my behalf—although they'd advised me not to join the reserves, convinced that I wouldn't be drafted. Heading now from the frying pan to the fire, I was hardened by their inertia.

My second appeal granted me new orders, and I reported to Fort MacArthur in Southern California awaiting a decision on my hardship discharge. I was just happy someone had read one of the letters. Growing silently optimistic, I could still hear that distant clock ticking.

I was still on leave when my sister, Pat, told me in confidence that my mom was unable to continue the house payments, and foreclosure was on the horizon. Her job simply paid her too little. I knew that we'd lose our house if I couldn't be discharged. Nothing seemed to make sense. Here I was being drafted to serve my duty abroad, and the army was taking me away from my duty at home. That thought made me one angry American. . . .

Finally, the dreaded day came—none of my appeals were granted, and I was on my way to San Francisco for what could be immediate deployment.

⇜ ⇜ ⇜

I tried to keep up with the Dodgers through all of this, but the '67 season turned out to be one of the franchise's poorest ever. They finished 28.5 games out of first place—the Dodgers' worst finish since relocating. Some sportswriters were saying that the Dodgers never fully recovered from the Orioles' sweep in the '66 Series. Sandy Koufax was no longer there either, and the team's pitching staff was diminished significantly.

I watched the World Series that year, fought between the Red Sox and the Cardinals, from my army barracks. I only rooted for the Red Sox, which went against my grain, because I knew one of their pitchers, Jerry Stephenson, since high school. His father, Joe, had first introduced me to Ted Williams in '61. Jerry did get to play, but in a game that was decided before he took the mound. The Cardinals were already up 6-0 behind the flawless pitching of Bob Gibson, winning Game 4 to give them a 3-2 edge over the Sox. Game 5 went to Boston thanks to a gem from pitcher Jim Lonborg. The Series headed back to Boston for Game 6, and the Sox's bats came to life, winning 8-4. Boston wished to shed the "Curse of the Bambino" by capturing the championship in Game 7.

So now the scene was set for the seventh and deciding game. Boston's comeback victory seemed to indicate that the emotional pendulum had swung in their favor. Playing at home to a sell-out crowd, Boston was looking to finally break the curse by winning its first World Series since trading Babe Ruth to the New York Yankees, but Bob Gibson was too much, and the Cardinals won the decider, 7-2.

The Series' end brought my military obligations back to the forefront, and as Thanksgiving approached, I was more depressed than ever. Fortunately, some of us met a nice couple who invited us for a Thanksgiving dinner, which they tried to do each year with the local servicemen. That wonderful meal turned out to be my last before deployment, and that couple showed us the true meaning of Thanksgiving through kindness and generosity on that special evening. Their faces reflected our fears, and their compassion was obvious as we left them that night knowing that we might never see them again. For some of us that happened to be the case.

≈ ≈ ≈

All of the practical options of delaying my departure were exhausted. Everything was "in process," but nowhere near an answer. My attorney offered some off-the-record advice, telling me that I should "disappear for a while," so for two and a half days, I stayed off-base hoping news would arrive.

That news did arrive—in the form of three military policemen (MPs). While at a local nightspot in Oakland, I was met by two MPs at my table, informed that a third waited outside.

"Are you PFC Gleason?" One asked.

"Yes."

"We have orders for you to return to base immediately, and we're here to escort you."

"Can you show me the papers?" I asked.

"Sir, you'll have all your papers when you reach the base. Please come with us."

I quickly finished my drink and followed them out the door. On the ride back, I remembered that the day started cold and cloudy, progressing to a heavy rain that evening. I never liked rain. Growing up in Southern California, I'd grown used to the sunshine, and the incessant rain depressed me even further. I felt like the weather was mirroring my mood. I was heading to hell after a short stay in heaven.

Once we got to the base, I was told to assemble all of my belongings, pack them, and prepare to board a bus en route to Travis Air Force Base. Everything became foggy from there, and I hardly remember the bus ride to Travis, but I'll never forget what happened when we arrived. We were given some private time before taking off, so I called my family and friends. I called my mother and sisters, but the telephone rang and rang, and I realized no one was home. I hung up the telephone, and fell against the wall of the phone booth, dejected—I couldn't even say what could be my last goodbye to the people I loved most.

I made my last call to Kenny Myers, who'd played such an important part in my life.

"Hello?"

"Kenny? It's Roy."

"Roy! Where are you?"

"I'm at Travis Air Force Base. You probably won't be hearing from me for a while, because I'm headed for Vietnam."

"Christ . . . how are you holding up?"

I called him at dinnertime, and he seemed distant. Maybe he remembered telling me not to worry about the draft, that the Dodgers would take care of me. I was hoping for some fatherly advice from a man I truly considered able to deliver such wisdom.

"Roy, I don't know what to tell you, but there are times when we all have to do what we have to do. . . ."

Before hanging up, he wished me "good luck." I'd never felt so empty. The wind blew my sulking frame back into the phone booth as the cold rain battered my face.

The Day My Life Changed Forever

"Welcome aboard! You'll be happy to know that you'll be flying first class on the top airline to the Far East," said an air force jokester as we boarded the plane.

"What airline is that?" A guy behind me asked.

"'Tiger Airlines,' non-stop to Hawaii, the Philippines, Guam—also called the 'Island of Pleasure'—and all points east!"

I could tell that some of the young GIs thought the trip wasn't going to be bad at all, but it didn't take long to learn that it was all bullshit. We were stopping for gas, not for pleasure. As we took off, my mind cycled through the events of the past few months and hours. I worried that my mother and sisters would be homeless. I thought of my friends, Gary and Wazy, who were en route to Europe—and I longed to join them. I wondered if I'd ever see America again, if I'd play for the Dodgers, if my dream was nothing but a distant memory.

As the city lights of St. Francis receded into the distance, I concentrated on the darkness and uncertainty that awaited me. I was the *only* GI without his sealed personal records sending him to Vietnam. I was told while boarding that they'd catch up with me or arrive before I did. Technically, I could've refused to board the plane, and now I felt even more helpless, depressed, and angry.

When speaking with former players and coaches for this book, I learned some very interesting information about the Dodgers. Apparently, three of my teammates had also been reclassified, and the Dodgers had protected them by making sure they entered the reserves, thereby avoiding the draft. Those three players never went to Vietnam. In my case, however, the Dodgers told me to stay away from the reserves. Of course, I was a grown man and could've made that decision for myself, but the fact that I didn't only fueled my resentment and anger.

I glanced over the faces of the young men accompanying me to hell and wondered, "What dreams did they forsake, and how many of us will live to see them come true?"

12
Going to the Front

D ecember 21, 1967—As I stepped off the plane, the sweet smell of orange blossoms was absent, replaced instead by the suffocating scent of burning oil and garbage. Along with 200 new recruits eager to touch land, I'm sure we looked like schoolchildren on a field trip to the veteran soldiers. Due to heavy shelling, we were unable to land at our intended destination, Saigon, so our plane was rerouted to Long Bin. Just before we landed, I noticed that the jungle landscape looked more like the surface of the moon from all the bomb craters.

Throughout the trip, every one of us was on edge, but we tried to keep things upbeat—but in our minds we feared the future. We'd all seen the pictures of body bags and flag-draped coffins, and none of us wanted to talk about that. We were young men—our entire lives lay ahead of us. Most of us slept through the trip, trying hard to forget the days ahead and dream of the people we loved. The pockets of turbulence we met en route reminded me of the bumpy uncertainty of life, and I couldn't help but wonder which men were sleeping under their guardian angels—and who rested under the veil of death's angel. We were told that casualties would come, but the enemy would experience 100 times more. Somehow, that didn't make any of us feel any better, and the reality quickly sank in that we might never come home.

~ ~ ~

Back home, the war remained the main topic in politics and households. George Romney, Michigan's governor, withdrew his name as a Republican candidate for president because he felt the war was a tragic mistake. Once a proponent of the war, he felt like he'd been brainwashed by the military and politicians when visiting Vietnam in '65. People were paying attention now, and dominoes were falling. Defense secretary Robert McNamara ominously resigned his position, and some felt that Pentagon hard-liners were behind his departure. History indicates that McNamara opposed bombing North Vietnam, but not sending more troops. We all thought it ironic and unfair that the man could leave his job after sticking all of us in the jungle to do his.

Senator Eugene McCarthy of Minnesota was challenging President Johnson's reelection, becoming the first "peace candidate." He claimed that Vietnam had created a "moral crisis in America."

"The Johnson administration has set no limit to the price that it is willing to pay for military victory," he said.

(Is history repeating itself today?)

Protest against the war intensified from coast to coast. In October '67, thousands of people congregated outside the Pentagon, and the peaceful group grew violent as tempers flared. Similar incidents occurred in San Francisco, Los Angeles, New York, and Madison (Wisconsin) during the same month.

I was never a student of politics nor was I interested in what our government was doing in the world. But I had mixed emotions about the protesters. The war started under noble pretenses, and I was taught to aid people in need. I think that's what we were doing in Vietnam, and that's what we're doing today. I've always been competitive, and trying your best isn't always enough for me. We fought Vietnam without a commitment to victory. My father always told me, "When you fight a war, you do whatever is necessary to win." We were fighting from a strictly defensive stance, and because of that, the Vietnam conflict was unraveling as the longest military war in U.S. history. The protestors were exercising their freedoms, but I thought that they might have given the enemy strength by their actions—they knew we were divided at home, and they capitalized on that fact. I believe it was President Lincoln who said, "All the armies of the world cannot prevail against America, but if America is to fall, it will be because of division within. . . ."

I remember my father and grandfather discussing one time that America has never been an imperialist country. They reasoned that we proved that in the wake of WWII, when we could've controlled the globe since we alone possessed the atomic bomb. We weren't in Vietnam to take over, but to prevent the communists from taking over.

⌇ ⌇ ⌇

December in Vietnam didn't bring the Christmas to which I was accustomed. Instead, we were in Vietnam's monsoon season and spending most of our time at Bearcat, our base camp. Flaming barrels containing human waste lined the paths to our quarters, called a "hooch," where some noncom-jerks (noncommissioned officers) were in charge. The noncoms would play mind games to initiate us to our new surroundings. We'd all be relaxing, and some moron would yell, "Incoming!" Instantly, we'd grab our mattresses and cover ourselves on the floor. We could hear the mortars, but they were outward-bound, and the vets would laugh their asses off as we put our beds back together. Soon we learned the difference between incoming and outgoing mortars by sound, and believe me—there's a huge difference.

Since I still lacked my official paperwork, I reported to the CO immediately to let them know that I was awaiting word on a hardship discharge. Of course, he told me, "You're not the only one. We'll let you know." I inquired about my military records, which were lost somewhere in the appropriate channels, but no answer came there, either. I looked over my special orders, dated December 20, 1967, and noticed that I was listed with no dependents. How could the army miss that? I had my mother and younger sister to support. I headed back to the office and showed them the mistake.

"Are you married?"

"No, sir."

"'Dependents' means 'children,' Private. Since you're not married and have no children, you have no dependents."

"But I'm the only person supporting my mother and youngest sister, sir."

"I'm sorry, Private. That's just not how it works."

Since I didn't have my official records, I received only partial pay ($50 per month), which was only a third of what I should've received. ($150 per month was standard combat pay.) I had told my mom I'd send her most of the money I'd make, but even in 1967, $50 didn't go very far, and I could only send $25. I was convinced the entire goddamn world was caving directly onto me.

Although I hoped my appeals would come through, I realized that I needed to adapt to the reality of war—and my position right in the middle of it all. Part of the learning process includes talking with soldiers who've recently returned from the front. What we learned is that men were dying in droves because we were often outnumbered. We were fighting a defensive war, which gave the enemy easy opportunities to find us. We didn't know the face of our enemy, either, which made the situation even more deadly. The truth is, no typical "front line" ever existed. We'd hear that the enemy had taken a position in a delta area, so we'd go out in choppers, but encounter minimal resistance. After returning to base, we'd learn the same area was again in enemy control. The army had no idea what they were doing in Vietnam. We were strangers in a strange land, perpetually on our heels. Our "prime directive," as it was called, was to make contact with the enemy. "Do not fire unless fired upon," was our basic rule as we patrolled areas in the Mekong Delta region, which was comprised of rice paddies, elephant grass, and dense jungle. Our paranoia extended to young children and women, who would hide weapons or even sacrifice themselves for the enemy.

"Never take the same trail twice" was another rule—one that would be broken later.

≈ ≈ ≈

Once in Vietnam, we learned that casualty counts were much higher than we'd previously thought. Of our original company of 99 men, only one person escaped Vietnam wound-free. Steve Mallory truly had a guardian angel hovering over him. Half of the men we arrived with never returned, and of those who did, 99 percent were wounded at some point.

When we arrived as Green Peas (new arrivals), we had no idea what was about to happen. The enemy was planning the Tet Offensive to coincide with the Vietnamese lunar new year. We were told that we arrived just in time, and we wondered, as Christmas came and went, whether it'd be our last. I reflected upon my turbulent life as the New Year approached, and thought to myself, "How did I go from Vero Beach to Vietnam in nine months?"

Many myths existed in the public consciousness about Vietnam, and movies may perpetuate many of those same myths today.[1] One of those myths is that the war was fought by youths, not men. The average age of Americans killed in Vietnam was approximately 23 years old. Eleven percent of those killed were over 30 years old, and the oldest serviceman killed was 62. I was 24 when I arrived, and I can say that I saw men die who were both younger and older than I was.

Another myth is that officers stayed behind the lines in Saigon, and the enlisted men fought the war. Officers accounted for almost 14 percent of casualties, and 12 generals died in the war—far more than the percentage of officer corps lost in WWII. I experienced these losses firsthand within months of my arrival. Furthermore, many believe that only the poorly educated served in Vietnam. But over 80 percent of the troops had high school diplomas (compared to 65 percent of the American public at the time), and three times as many college graduates served in Vietnam than in WWII.

Those men, who enlisted, served, and perhaps died in Vietnam, were some of the greatest fighting men and heroes this nation has ever known. They were fighting with one hand tied behind them, but they believed that we could save South Vietnam from communist control, and educated or not, they laid down their lives for that belief.

Only one-third of our troops came from the draft, compared to two-thirds in WWII. Volunteers accounted for 77 percent of those killed in action, and less than one percent of KIAs were 18-year-old draftees. Each man accompanying me from Travis Air Force Base had been drafted, and we knew we were facing the very real possibility of death.

⤬ ⤬ ⤬

Christmas Day 1967 found most of us beginning the day by attending church. I'm not what you would call a church person, but I wanted to be there on that day. The mood was still somewhat somber due to our circumstances, but the chaplain led us in familiar Christmas carols, and for a few minutes, I felt like I was home. I said some prayers that morning, and the chaplain's sermon ended on a positive note—that our country prayed for the war to end and our safe return. We didn't leave the base or initiate combat that day, nor did we take any enemy fire, to my recollection.

"Too bad Christmas only comes once a year," I remember one soldier remarked, and I couldn't have agreed more—even when I was a child. The week between Christmas and New Year's contained a ton of activity, and the enemy was engaging us more often and with greater firepower.

I remember New Year's Day 1968 vividly, by comparing it to the one I had enjoyed a year earlier, when I was celebrating with friends and family, watching football and the Rose Parade on television. The only thing similar to that day was that it was warm, but nothing like the warmth of Southern California. This heat was sticky and filled with the roasted aroma of burning waste. On the Eve, we had our usual amount of sleep—three or four hours—and we were advised to expect enemy action. Although we later learned that some of our controlled areas fell under attack, things stayed fairly quiet around me. We shared a brief toast of beer, and although I don't remember the names of those men, I'll never forget their faces or that night.

On January 2, 1968, Armed Forces Radio played us a recording of the Rose Bowl, in which the University of Southern California defeated Indiana University. I tried to imagine the scene at home: Mom cooking in the kitchen, our family and friends surrounding the television. Did we even still have a home? The more I thought about it, the more concerned I became, and the more helpless I felt. Most guys' eyes would light up if you asked them about home, but I'd grow angry. When asked what was wrong, I'd always say, "It's a long story, and I'd rather not get into it. . . ."

Beginning that New Year, we all hoped and prayed that the war would end soon. We knew the days ahead would be filled with danger. None of us knew that we'd face the war's biggest test less than 30 days later.

---

[1] *The statistics come from* Stolen Valor, *by B.G. Burkett and Glenna Whitley (Verity Press— 1998).*

13

The Day Our Officers Died

All hell broke loose on January 31, 1968. The North Vietnamese launched their Tet Offensive, and according to most accounts, the war changed dramatically. Within 24 hours, the North had sent 84,000 fresh troops to attack every region in the South, caring little about civilian casualties along the way. I was there when they came.

The Viet Cong spent months planning the campaign. Apparently, they felt the major offensive would weaken any remaining morale that we still possessed, destroying the American resolve to continue its support. Since their aim included many urban areas in the South, civilians were caught in the crossfire often, and many innocent people lost their lives.

What many historical reports fail to mention is that the Tet Offensive was actually a military victory for U.S. forces. Although significantly outnumbered, we were able to defeat the enemy soundly and inflicted severe losses. In less than a week, the enemy lost over 50,000 men, and hundreds of thousands were wounded. The North had gained no territory, and American forces had delivered one of the most lopsided defeats in military history.

The myth still exists that the Tet Offensive was a victory for North Vietnamese forces, but it's simply not true. Perhaps our nation lost its resolve after eight years of bloody conflict—the longest in our history.

Roy stands atop a French fort in 1968. *From the Roy Gleason Collection*

The antiwar media persuaded the American public to believe that our enemy was superior and more dedicated, but the people were misled. Two months later, Walter Cronkite of *CBS News* broke the journalist's code, recognizing the war as ". . . futile and immoral," and he said a recent trip to Vietnam left him ". . . deeply disillusioned."

I didn't understand his position. Was he saying that fighting communism was "futile and immoral"? Did he believe that walking away would strengthen our position against the communists? What did he think would happen to the South Vietnamese people once we packed up and left? History showed us the brutality that followed. . . .

Later that same month we learned that our own commander in chief, Lyndon B. Johnson, had announced that he would not be seeking reelection. Saying that the war had ". . . created a division in the American house," now even he was bailing on us.

Obviously, this affected each of us negatively. Unless you were there, you can't understand what it's like to place your life on the line for what seemed like ungrateful people and a questionable cause. How can someone understand the feeling of seeing your buddy's head blown off by a VC mine only to read about an American student calling the VC patriotic and his own countrymen the enemy? Let me tell you: We were disgusted. All the rats were jumping ship, and we were left to steer the wreckage to shore.

Perhaps that's why global leaders don't actually fear war. They'll never have to fight it, and they know it. How many wars do you think would be fought if two leaders had to fight to the death on a deserted island?

≈ ≈ ≈

I n January of '68 I was stationed at Fort Courage, an old French fort, which was located against the China Sea. Fort Courage was a massive concrete structure adorned with gun turrets, strategically positioned so that a few men could fend off a large attacking force. Just inland from the fort, all areas were infested with VC, and we were

Roy pauses at Fort Courage in 1968. *From the Roy Gleason Collection*

constantly under mortar attack—although those attacks amounted to little given our superior firepower and air support. All of that changed in one violent moment.

The French constructed the fort in 1910 using tons of mortar and concrete—the building was so sturdy that mortars sounded like a piece of hail in a rainstorm. When the smoke cleared, nothing had changed, which probably pissed Charlie off severely. During one of the evening attacks, our company's officers wanted to call in artillery and air support and put an end to the continuous menace. All six officers assembled on the top deck to pinpoint the enemy's location by searching for muzzle flashes. While they were scanning the night, the same deck took a direct hit, killing five of them instantly. The sixth officer, our forward observer (FO), lost his leg, and was evacuated immediately.

The attack left our company without any commanding officers—a state that remained for some time. As a result of the attack, First Sergeant Johnson, whom we called "Top," became our CO. Due to this catastrophe, my age, training, and classification thrust me into a leadership position, and I had to assume a lieutenant's role until a commissioned officer arrived as a replacement. What makes this entire event so tragic is that it never should have happened.

Military training and procedures dictate that officers are never to congregate in the same combat area or proximity in order to avoid this exact scenario. In this particular instance, those men forgot their training, and it cost them their lives. By making that careless decision, they put the entire company at risk since they left us without any trained officers to lead us. Seeing our commanding officers killed instantly brought the reality of war much closer that night. After that, sleep was a precious commodity, but it was never sound, and we all wondered which sniper's bullet or enemy mortar had our name on it.

While in charge of my platoon (which consisted of around 25 men), I followed my training and kept our unit together. We continued our "search and destroy" missions and initiated contact with the enemy. I assured my men that we'd get through it, but we needed to work together more than ever. Our men became far more cooperative and dedicated than they had been under our COs—more than ever, our lives depended on it. Instead of a chicken with its head cut off, we rose to the occasion and soared.

Central Command knew of our losses and immediately began to call up young officers right out of Officer Candidates School (OCS). The obvious problem was that these men were completely inexperienced, and that didn't sit well with any of us. As soon as they arrived, they were placed in charge, but they knew very little about what was happening. They soon learned, and news of their predecessors' demise may have expedited that process.

～ ～ ～

Due to the circumstances and an earlier campaign, I was nominated for the Bronze Star, signifying my "service with distinction and valor under fire." As a result of those two events, I was recognized by the army as "Soldier of the Month" for June 1968 in the publication *Stars and Stripes*, which earned me several weeks as the commanding general's bodyguard. For the first time since my arrival, I was not on the front lines. My security classification was upgraded, and I had a chance to see a completely different side of combat and the entire war.

The earlier campaign was a mission in Vietnam's southern regions, near what is called the "Plain of Reeds." It was March of '68, and we were on another search and destroy mission. We were flown into the delta region by chopper in late afternoon. The region itself is known for its wild, tall reeds, dense vegetation, and intermingled rice paddies. The reeds grow so thick that they cut your skin as you pass through them. The ground is always swampy due to the Mekong Delta, and pockets of deadly quicksand lurk beneath the surface everywhere.

Once we landed, we fanned out, positioning ourselves with other platoons in the rice paddy. From the dense jungle that surrounded us, small-arms fire emerged, and then all hell broke loose. We returned fire, but the enemy was standing their ground instead of firing and retreating. To my right, a soldier took a bullet to the gut and dropped. I quickly crawled to him, tossed him over my shoulder as a fireman does, and carried him to safety under a large dike. I called for a medic, but I could tell that he was seriously wounded.

As I crawled to the dike's peak, I saw another soldier drop to the ground, his knee obliterated by a machine-gun shell. As I slithered towards him, I could tell that he was losing tons of blood. I quickly tied a tourniquet around his upper leg.

"I'll get you to the dike area," I screamed over gunshots. "You'll be safe there."

In June 1968 at Bearcat, Ninth Infantry division headquarters, Roy was selected as "Soldier of the Month" for his division. He receives awards from division commanders, a sergeant major on the left, and Major General Julian Ewell on the right. *From the Roy Gleason Collection*

I managed to pick him up and carry him to safety with the other wounded soldier. My guardian angel was with me. I could hear and feel shells flying by, and one pierced my helmet, nicking my skull and drawing blood. Our platoon leader called in artillery and aerial gun ships to rake the area, which they soon did—some of their fire hitting our position as well.

I realized that I'd dropped my rifle and the wounded soldiers' weapons in the muddy ambush zone, so I crawled out into danger once more, and in that moment, I could see the bullets coming toward me in slow motion, tearing up the earth all around me. Once I reached my rifle, I scuttled back to a moat and returned fire.

Although the firefight was the longest I'd experienced to that point, I was far more worried about the two wounded men. After our gun ships had quelled the enemy fire, it took almost an hour for Medivac choppers to arrive. To this day, I don't know if those men survived that day, and although I never learned their names, their faces are permanently engraved in my mind.

≈ ≈ ≈

Even though I was in the thick of war, I'd still sometimes think about the Dodgers and how much I missed playing baseball. I received many letters from home, which kept me updated on the latest, kept my dreams in tact, and kept my morale high enough to survive.

I wondered about '68 spring training and if I could help the Dodgers rebound from a lousy showing in '67. I couldn't help feeling that I really needed to be there instead of sitting in the God-forsaken land of Vietnam. Five seasons had passed since I'd played in the majors, and I wasn't getting any younger. Here I was dodging bullets each day, fighting a war that half our nation opposed, and I hadn't heard one word from the Dodger brass or Kenny Myers. To say I was discouraged doesn't begin to touch the surface.

The only bright spot during that period was that Buzzie Bavasi, the Dodgers' general manager, and some Dodger Boosters sent me a package. Enclosed was information about the Dodgers and their minor league clubs so I could follow many of my former teammates' progress. While I appreciated the effort, I wished he'd sent more—it also would've been great to hear from some of those teammates as well. The Boosters' letters were from fans, and they took their time to write a person they didn't know. Each letter included that I was missed and in their prayers—little did they know how much that meant to me at that time. They also sent clippings to let me know about developments during the season.

One particular clipping caught my attention more than any other. The same month that I was named "Soldier of the Month," Don Drysdale set the National League record of scoreless innings pitched at 58 2/3 innings, breaking Walter Johnson's record of 56 from 1913. I couldn't have been happier for Don, who was always a good friend to me, but I was depressed that I didn't get to see it. With Sandy Koufax's sudden departure in '66, Don was carrying an unfair load upon his shoulders, but he definitely rose to the occasion.

Unfortunately, '68 doesn't remind me of Don's excellence, but rather of the lives that were lost that year—in combat and on the home front. In April of '68, Martin Luther King was murdered, resulting in riots throughout the country. All of us wondered, "What the hell is happening in America?" We had no idea things would get worse.

Two months later, Senator Robert Kennedy was shot after winning the California Democratic presidential primary, just five years after his brother met a similar fate. Bobby Kennedy campaigned with the platform of ending the war, and an assassin silenced him.

Even though we were shocked and saddened by these heinous events, we ended that day with another night of search and destroy—no matter what happened at home, we were still fighting a war. My mind was unusually clear, though, and it all dates back to May, before any of the assassinations. An event occurred that would change my life, and I felt, for the first time, that I would not leave the battlefields in a body bag or return home in a flag-draped coffin.

14

"The Bench" and My Guardian Angel

To this day, I don't consider myself a religious person. My mother made sure that I received some religious training and education as a young boy, raising me as a Lutheran. When I was young, we attended church each Sunday without fail, and I attended Sunday school, and years later I tried to go on a fairly regular basis. When we moved to Garden Grove, it didn't take my mom long to find St. Paul's Lutheran Church, which was presided over by the aforementioned Pastor Weirsig.

Pastor Weirsig always encouraged me to follow my dreams, and he labored to see that I wasn't drafted (a labor of love, but not success). I know that he often told my mother he was very proud of me when he read that I'd signed with the Dodgers. After high school, my mother would tell me that he'd ask about me all the time.

"Tell him I'll be watching when they call him up," he'd tell her.

In '63, when I was called up and played, I don't know if any of those games were televised, but I promise that he saw them if they were. He always showed that he cared about me, never more than by his efforts to convince the draft board to reconsider my reclassification. He was one of the few people who kept in contact after I went to Vietnam as well. Pastor Weirsig was a very special person, an eloquent speaker, a true friend, and a real man of God. I'll never forget him or what he did for me.

Anyway, I believe that Pastor Weirsig was responsible for my adult understanding of God, and I believe that the Good Lord has answered many of my prayers throughout my life—including signing a professional contract with the Dodgers. I'm also sure He's been disappointed with me on many occasions, and sometimes I wondered whether my time in Vietnam was meant as purgatory. I think it was my mother who told me, "God has a plan for you." I thought that perhaps He was testing me—and if that's the case, I learned an important lesson: life is a fleeting moment. Yet nothing that I'd experienced in my life to that point compared with what was about to happen to me in Vietnam.

I understand that accepting what I'm about to tell you will be difficult. You'll disbelieve because it defies logic and scientific explanation, and perhaps due to the circumstances, you'll write it off as a figment of my imagination. With God as my witness, however, I was not inebriated or high or temporarily insane, and what happened does defy all practical interpretation. I can assure you that I do believe in God, in miracles, in the supernatural, and in "guardian angels." And on that May night in Vietnam, something supernatural saved my life.

After my brief week of rest and relaxation in Hong Kong, I was back to the front, where I learned that our company had been reassigned to Roch Kien—an inland base camp in the delta region. We stayed in bunkers made of sandbags and mud, and the air was so stuffy that no one could sleep. At night, those bunkers were infested with man-eating mosquitoes—as big as butterflies, malarial, and hungry. We'd crap for three days at a time after our orange-pill Mondays, but you quickly learn that dying from malaria is far worse than a bullet to the head. In order to buy ourselves a brief respite, we'd often toss smoke bombs into the bunkers to kill the bugs. Sometimes I'd sleep outside, which was better for the bugs, but we were taking around 400 mortar rounds per night, so that threat was far more serious.

On this particular night, I decided to sleep on an old, wooden bench that I'd slept on many times. Around 4:00 a.m., I felt something picking me up, moving me off the bench towards the bunker. You never sleep soundly in combat, so I was instantly awake. Something was pushing me from behind, and I didn't see anyone or anything anywhere. I saw the bunker approaching quickly, and the next thing I knew, I was crashing into the bunker, onto a cot near the L-shaped opening. A force that I never saw threw me into the air and onto that cot.

Obviously, you're thinking, "It was someone or maybe more than one person who grabbed him, and he was still sleeping. . . ." Well, I saw no one, felt no hands. Some may think that it was the concussion of a nearby mortar explosion, but that didn't happen, either. When I landed on that cot, there had been no preceding noise or explosions—it was silent. I was lying on the cot wondering, "What the hell just happened?"

And that's when everything changed, and all hell broke loose. As I was looking towards the opening of the bunker, searching the darkness for whom or what had transplanted me, a blinding flash and concussion blast shook everyone awake, rattling the bunker walls. That shell hit the bench I was sleeping on with pinpoint accuracy, blowing it into a million splinters. None of my company was out or awake before this, so no one had thrown me into the bunker. Perhaps you may think that a sympathetic Vietnamese saved me, but that was not it—nor was it a dream. We received around 300 mortar rounds that night, and some unknown force moved me to safety, saving my life.

To this day, I think it was my guardian angel.

Who is my guardian angel? God only knows, but I think it could be my departed grandfather, who knew I was in immediate danger. I had never experienced anything like that before nor since, and I'm hesitant to disclose this now, but I know what happened, and I'm here today to tell about it.

Minutes after the dust cleared, we didn't have time to talk about it—we were just grateful to still be standing. After the attack, I went over to the area where I'd been sleeping and found a large hole sprinkled with splinters. The only footprints I could find were my own. As I continued to search for evidence, I was shocked to find nothing. I asked everyone in my unit, but no one admitted to the rescue. Everyone said they were asleep, and no one had noticed any strangers around camp.

Before any of this happened, I wasn't very confident that I'd make it out of hell alive; but now, because of the "bench experience," all that changed. I couldn't find an excuse to keep me there.

For the first time, I felt that something supernatural was protecing me from death.

≈ ≈ ≈

Around that same time, peace talks opened between the U.S. and North Vietnam in Paris, perhaps due to the lack of a military success for either side. We all hoped and prayed for peace, but the war kept dragging on without any change. Our only reality was pain and death. We learned later that both sides spent several weeks arguing about the *size* of the conference table—people were dying, and they were arguing over the size of a goddamned table.

15
Recovering

From May 7-12, 1968, the VC launched another intensive offensive, and just before my near-death bench experience, we were flown to a bridge outside Saigon with orders to prevent its capture. Although peace talks had begun, it seemed that no one had told Charlie. We were without a moment to relax, and we continued to become demoralized by the lack of public support at home. That sentiment seemed to give the enemy greater hope and confidence, and if they could just hold on, they were sure we'd pack up and leave.

The best thing coming from the States was the mail, and I was still receiving cards and letters from family and friends. Buzzie Bavasi continued to send me information about the organization and players, which kept my hopes alive of returning to the diamond. Still I hadn't received any letters from Kenny Myers, or—perhaps more debilitating—from my father. Although my parents were divorced, I always thought that he'd be the one to write if I went to war—after all, he'd served in WWII, so he knew what it was like and how important correspondence was to the soldier. But I never received a letter from him—not one.

DEPARTMENT OF THE ARMY
HEADQUARTERS 9TH INFANTRY DIVISION
APO San Francisco 96370

GENERAL ORDERS   3 November 1968
NUMBER   10401

AWARD OF THE ARMY COMMENDATION MEDAL FOR HEROISM

1. TC 320. The following AWARD is announced.

GLEASON, ROY W. US56704936 ▓▓▓▓▓▓▓▓▓ SERGEANT E5 United States
Army, Company A, 3rd Battalion, 39th Infantry, 9th Infantry Division, APO
96371
Awarded: Army Commendation Medal with "V" Device
Date action: 24 July 1968
Theater: Republic of Vietnam
Reason: For heroism in connection with military operations involving con-
         flict with an armed hostile force in the Republic of Vietnam:
         Sergeant Gleason distinguished himself on 24 July 1968 while
         serving as Squad Leader with Company A, 3rd Battalion, 39th
         Infantry, on a reconnaissance in force mission near Fire Support
         Base Lambert. After receiving wounds from an enemy land mine,
         Sergeant Gleason refused medical aid and continued to perform his
         duties as Squad Leader until all his wounded men had been evacuated.
         Sergeant Gleason's heroic actions are in keeping with the highest
         traditions of the military service and reflect great credit upon
         himself, the 9th Infantry Division and the United States Army.
Authority: By direction of the Secretary of the Army under the provisions
            of AR 672-5-1, and USARV message 16695, dated 1 July 1966.

FOR THE COMMANDER:

OFFICIAL: IRA A. HUNT, JR.
                                     COL, GS
                                     Chief of Staff

GEORGE W. WELLS, JR.
CPT, AGC
Asst AG

DISTRIBUTION: SPECIAL DISTRIBUTION:
  1-ASD   2-USA Pers Svc Support Center, ATTN: AGPE-F
  5-(5) ea indiv conc   Fort Benjamin Harrison, Indiana 46216
  1-(1) ea indiv 201 file   22-TOTAL
  2-PIO
  2-AVDE-MH (19th MHD)
  2-Co A, 3rd Bn, 39th Inf
  2-CG USARV ATTN: AVHAG-PD
  5-Awds & Dec

The official order for Roy's Medal of Valor. *From the Roy Gleason Collection*

≈ ≈ ≈

Only seven weeks after the bench experience, my tour of duty
came to an end, when I was wounded by the same mortar that

killed Tony Sivo. I started my recovery in the field hospital in Saigon, where I was stuck for a week. I received my Purple Heart while a patient there—a bird colonel came to visit the wounded and mentioned that he was sorry for my wounds and assured me that my army and nation were proud and appreciative of my actions to preserve freedom. The entire ceremony was very simple—the colonel congratulated each of us and pinned the medal on our hospital pajamas. Although the ceremony wasn't extravagant, I knew that my sacrifice had been recognized—I was only worried that the sacrifice would include my baseball career. My grandfather and father often spoke of the Purple Heart, though, saying that it was awarded to the "bravest of the brave," and I was proud to carry that honor. My wounds were serious, and the doctors were not optimistic about my return to baseball, but I decided early on that I'd recover. I was convinced that the physical scars would heal, but the emotional scars would be there forever.

A week after being recognized, I was transferred to the 249th Hospital in Osaka, Japan, for two weeks. During that time, I was able to use a wheelchair, and I slowly rebuilt my strength. On August 15, I was transferred once again—to Letterman Hospital in San Francisco, California.

I was finally home.

⤸ ⤸ ⤸

At Letterman, I began an intensive physical therapy program to regain full use of my left arm and wrist, as well as my leg. Although painful, I still felt that things were moving too slow, but the doctors said that I was making exceptional progress. I told them that I was on a mission to return to baseball, but their faces told me that they had their doubts. After many weeks, I was regaining my strength and had moved from a cautious few steps to short sprints. I had seven months to prepare for spring training, and I knew that I couldn't afford to miss another season.

I mainly used my recovery to contemplate what I'd been through, and I remember going through two psychological stages. I was still very angry and resented the circumstances that had led me to that point, but I was also thankful to be alive. I prayed that God would help me get back into baseball, and that hope helped me put the past aside.

I also had a chance to renew my correspondence with Ted Williams as I recovered. I wrote Ted many months earlier from Vietnam after reading a *Sports Illustrated* article he wrote about the art of hitting. Much to my surprise, he wrote me back, and his letters took forever to get to me since I'd been returned to the States. He'd written twice, telling me in his last letter, ". . . Keep your ass down and get out of that rat hole ASAP." I didn't know if he remembered that day that I'd met him as a teenager at La Palma Park, and as I thought about that day, it seemed both very near and very far away.

All the letters I received were important to me, and I consider them personal treasures—but I had to laugh at one in particular. A letter arrived from the U.S. Army stating that my official records had been received, and they were pleased to inform me that I'd been granted full military compensation including combat pay. Talk about timing. . . . For almost eight months, I was dodging bullets and bombs at half pay. Had I received that pay, I could've helped save our house from foreclosure. I figured my hardship discharge would come in the mail within days. I couldn't have been more disappointed with our government and its inane bureaucracy.

I couldn't help feeling a certain degree of guilt from surviving my tour, knowing that some of my best friends did not. Why did Tony Sivo, Sergeant Long, and PFC Harton have to die? Why did so many other good men have to spend their last moments in that God-forsaken land while I was given the opportunity to go on? I began to have doubts about God's mercy—how could he send the good and courageous to death while allowing me and even cowards to live?

I tried to turn that negative energy into positive motivation in my mission to recover fully, which I would do, and I dedicated that rehabilitation to those I served with, those who gave their lives, and those who had always believed in me.

≈ ≈ ≈

L ooking back on the experience, I realize that I was given another chance to do great things on the ball field, and that inspiration fueled my desire to be ready for spring training, 1969. When I was in the hospital, some Dodger executives sent me some cards wishing a speedy recovery. The doctors gave me convalescence leave in late August for 30 days, which was the best news I'd received in a long time.

Jimmy Lefebvre, who was playing for the Dodgers, stopped by the hospital to see me before I left, and he was there when I received news of the release. He and his wife had driven to San Francisco so he could serve his two weeks in the National Guard Reserve, and they told me that Jimmy's wife could drive me to Los Angeles. He hated that she'd make the trip back alone anyway, so I couldn't turn him down. On the ride back, I couldn't help feeling slighted by the irony. The Dodgers convinced me not to join the National Guard, which Jimmy had done to avoid combat. I guess I was just plain stupid for listening to them. By following their advice, I missed two seasons and nearly lost my life.

Earlier that same day, I spoke with Dan Gentile, who was also recovering from combat wounds. Dan was in the 39th Infantry, but we weren't in the same company, so I didn't meet him until I got to Letterman. He had suffered what some call, "the million-dollar wound." A bullet had severed his index finger, but due to some quick thinking under fire, he saved it; and doctors were able to sew it together. We laughed for hours about that procedure, in which the doctors used a button to secure his nerves and tendons—so he had a button sewn onto his trigger finger. I used to tell him, "Make sure you don't get that finger stuck in your nose or anywhere else!" Since he also lived in Southern California, I invited him to ride with Jimmy's wife and me, and we left the next morning for for my sister Pat's home in Hacienda Heights.

My mom and Cathy had moved to Pat's when our Garden Grove home was sold to avoid foreclosure. When we arrived, my mother invited Dan and Jimmy's wife for dinner, and we sat down to her delicious home cooking. The homecoming was bittersweet, though—I was happy to be home, but bitter that we'd lost our old house. I tried to focus on the positives, eating well and working out. I wanted to improve my strength and frame of mind as spring training slowly gained on me. I knew that the clock was ticking louder than ever. Being home was truly the best medicine for my recovery, and having my family and friends around me was a psychological "pep pill." The mornings were never fresher; the sky was never bluer; the grass was never greener; and the smell and taste of any breakfast was never better than my first full day there. My anger and frustration over the war had begun to subside, as did the guilt syndrome that accompanied my survival. I was just thankful to be home and alive.

I was sure that Kenny Myers would contact me as soon as I got home, but unfortunately, he hadn't contacted my mother for months, and I could tell they were as disappointed as I was. A few weeks after getting home, I went to an American Legion baseball tournament in Anaheim. Sitting there with a group of scouts was none other than Kenny, watching young players on the same field he had first seen me play—déjà vu. Seeing him there was no surprise, since many future stars were no doubt playing.

With my arm still in a cast, and stitches still in my left leg, I limped towards him and smiled. We spoke briefly, and I could tell that he felt uncomfortable. He seemed distant and cold.

"I'm glad to see you, Roy. How are you feeling?"

"Stronger each day, Kenny. If everything continues at this pace, I will be ready for spring training in February."

"I hope you will be, Roy. I really do." With that, he turned his attention back to the diamond.

We spoke briefly throughout the game, and afterward, he invited me to a party in Anaheim that several scouts were attending. I welcomed the idea of anything fun, so I accepted. Although the party was anything but fun, it was definitely funny.

A man named Ruben, whose last name escapes me, was the host, and he was a former wrestler who knew many scouts and players. I remember that Rocky Colavito was there—Rocky started that season with the Dodgers before going to the Yankees. I doubt if what happened that evening affected his leaving the Dodgers, but I doubt he'd forget it. I think it all started with Kenny, who before long was the center of attention.

Normally, Kenny was "Mr. Quiet," never much of a talker—especially to strangers. He was a shy person, but that changed drastically after a few too many drinks. Kenny got into an argument with Ruben, our wrestling host who was much larger than the short and stocky Mr. Myers was. That didn't bother Kenny, though, who informed our host that he was a "master of judo," and that he'd easily take the wrestler in a match. Ruben laughed off Kenny's proposal, as did everyone else—until Kenny persisted to the point that Ruben decided to take him up on his challenge.

The next thing we know, they're going at each other in the middle of the apartment. In a split second, Kenny was flying over Ruben's shoulder, hitting the floor with a large thud. Everyone grew silent, and that's when I decided to jump into things. I grabbed Ruben around the neck, but he dispatched of me as easily as he'd done with Kenny. Apparently, my participation in the match didn't sit well with Ruben's friends, and the entire room broke into a brawl.

I'd only been back for a month, and here I was fighting. I still had stitches in my leg and my cast on, of course, which came in handy during the brawl. In a few minutes it was finished—just as the cops arrived. Kenny was still in the middle of the floor, bloodied, yelling, "I can still kick your ass!" at the host. The party was over, and we left the messy apartment immediately. Although no one was arrested, I'm not sure if anyone received a bill for the damages.

I knew that the doctors at Letterman wouldn't approve of my actions—nor would the Dodgers. Kenny and I agreed to keep it quiet.

"Don't worry, I'll be ready for spring training," I told him.

"You better be," he said with a smile as he drove away.

Kenny was still like a father to me, even though I hadn't seen or heard from him in months. As I learned on that bleak December day nearly a year before, sometimes "we have to do what we have to do."

I learned later, during the interview process for this book, that Kenny was extremely unhappy during his last years with the Dodgers. His daughter, Margie, said that he actually considered leaving the organization, although I could never tell. Apparently, it all began with his territory being cut in half upon his return from Japan, and he felt that was unfair since the Dodgers had encouraged him to go in the first place. He felt they were wrong, and that sentiment may have affected his involvement with me. He wasn't a writer, that's for sure. He'd tell me, "Writing letters is what a secretary's for." Kenny was educated, but I didn't feel that he enjoyed writing, and perhaps that's the reason why I didn't receive a letter while in Vietnam.

⤳ ⤳ ⤳

I recently learned that the Dodgers refused a trade that would've sent me to Kansas City while I was in Vietnam. From what I understand, Rosy Gilhousen, who'd offered me $100,000 to sign with the Angels in 1961, was working for the expansion-club Royals by then. Rosy convinced the Royals to go after me, but the Dodgers decided to protect me from the expansion draft.

Some years later, Bill Gleason, a well-known sportswriter from Chicago and no relation, did some aggressive research and wrote an article about my baseball career. The article claimed that I was the only person to have played in the major leagues and served on the frontlines in Vietnam. I'm very proud of that fact, and I'm glad to join the likes of Ted Williams and many others as representatives of both baseball and our nation's military.

I understand that many veterans dislike discussing their memories of war—it's much more of a nightmare than a memory for many. I've seen strong, brave men cry—particularly those who've participated or witnessed combat. Ask them about those with whom they served, those who paid the ultimate price, and tears will well instantly. The scars are there forever, and I know this firsthand. I have a beautiful niece, Reneé, who says she remembers that I was much more fun before I went to Vietnam, and that I had a great sense of humor. After I returned, she'd often ask her mother, "Why are Uncle Roy's eyes always so sad?"

Some say that eyes are the windows to the soul, so I'm sure she noticed. I never totally escaped what happened in those jungles, but I was even more determined to prove to the Dodgers that my best years were still ahead of me. Something happened between my return and my recovery that created a desire I'd never known, and that event made the upcoming season of '69 the most challenging and important of my baseball career.

16

A Surprising and Special Night

O n a Friday in mid-September, Frank Worth invited me to stay at his Hollywood home instead of going to my sister's house for a visit. I flew home on the weekends to get away from Letterman, and I was feeling much stronger, although I still had shrapnel in my leg and a cast on my arm. When Frank heard that I'd been wounded, he was the first to call me while I was in the Japanese hospital to wish me well, and I told him that I'd contact him when I got to San Francisco.

"Your situation could make you a hot commodity in Hollywood, Roy," he'd tell me.

"I don't want to talk about Vietnam, though—I just want to forget about it. Besides, how many 'hot commodity' Vietnam vets do you know?"

"I guess I don't know of any, but that's why your story will catch on."

"That's beside the point. . . . I just want to move on with my baseball career, not think about hell."

From time to time, we'd discuss the war, and he seemed very interested in my firsthand perspective.

"We shouldn't be there—I think we're losing the war," Frank would say.

"Some damned politicians call Vietnam, 'a police action, not a war.' That's bullshit, Frank. It was a war, and it has cost over 50,000 American lives."

Since many people contended that we had no moral right to be there, we were losing the war? I've never accepted that for many reasons. First, the war lasted twice as long as WWII. Secondly, the enemy losses were staggering—over one million soldiers killed in action. Lastly, had we been committed at home, we would have prevailed in half the time, and red communism may have ended 10 years earlier than it did. That lack of commitment made us leave the battlefield—pure and simple.

"Our goal was never to occupy Vietnam, so you tell me who really won the war after hearing those statistics," I told Frank. Although he respected my views, I'm not sure that he understood or shared any of them.

Nonetheless, Frank was a great guy, so I agreed to stay at his home after putting him off while I regained my comfort level. He wanted to take me to a Dodgers game, which I joyfully agreed to do. We went to his home in the Hollywood Hills. Because of Frank's work in entertainment, he was always in the company of many attractive ladies, and this day was no different. He introduced me to many women looking to, as he put it, ". . . further their careers in show business." Those girls enjoyed the company of baseball players, and Frank had an eye for beauty. You can probably understand why I usually enjoyed hanging out with him. . . . I say, "usually," because after I returned, I didn't feel as comfortable, and I never wanted to put a damper on the evening.

I had evaded his previous invitations, and I knew that he sensed my reluctance. So he called me up while I was still in Letterman.

"What you need is to get out, see some girls, start socializing again, Roy. . . . I'm the official representative of the Ideal Medicine Company, and ol' Dr. Frank is prescribing a night on the town!"

I agreed, feeling much better, and on this particular occasion, Frank reintroduced me to Heidi Park, whom I first met in Vietnam when she came with the USO. The USO shows were very important to the troops—for a couple hours, we could forget about the war and the insanity and get a glimpse of *home*. Each of the talented entertainers let us know that we weren't forgotten at home. They provided a tremendous morale booster. I know that Bob Hope did many shows, but unfortunately, I never had the opportunity to see him. I met Johnny Grant at the USO show I attended because I was "Soldier of the Month," and I was protecting our commanding general, and Johnny introduced me to Heidi (me and about 3,000 other troops). I was also introduced to many Hollywood showgirls. A few months later, many of those same showgirls visited me in Letterman.

Frank was right about one thing—he had the "ideal medicine," and her name was Heidi. On that Friday in Hollywood, I spent some very enjoyable time with her—times that I still have fond memories of today.

On Saturday morning, Frank and I went to his favorite breakfast spot, Denny's.

"Have you given any thought to getting back into television and film, Roy? The off-season is the perfect chance for you. When you're released from Letterman, you need to call me."

"Sure, I guess. . . . You know that my main goal is getting back into playing shape for spring training, though."

"I know, Roy—baseball will always be your mistress."

After breakfast, I went to spend some more quality time with Heidi, and then Frank took me to the evening game at Dodger Stadium. The weather was beautiful—a perfect Southern California day. As we entered the empty clubhouse, I ran into Don Drysdale, who was very happy to see me.

"I heard about your record-breaking night while I was on the front, Don. Congratulations! That's an unbeatable mark!"

"Thanks, Roy," he said with a grin. "My arm's getting tired, though. How are you doing?"

He pointed to my arm cast. "I heard you were wounded. . . ."

"The doctors think I will make a full recovery," I told him. "I'll see you in spring training."

Shaking my hand, he said, "Think about pitching maybe, and you can take over for me."

Laughing, I wished him luck, and followed him and Frank through the stadium tunnel to the field, where the Dodgers were taking batting practice. After saying hello to many of the guys I'd known from before the war, I was introduced to many of the new players. The field looked fantastic, and I felt the excitement building inside of me as fans poured into the stadium, and I caught the sensory elements of the game: cigar smoke, freshly cut grass, hot dogs, and popcorn.

Here I was, back in what to me was a cathedral—a holy place where legends, saints, and sinners met on the field of competition. Only two months earlier, I was on another field—the battlefield—half a world away, where death was commonplace, and it smelled like hell. I saw the smiling faces of the fans, kids waving their gloves in the air, and my emotions welled. Teenage boys in the crowd may have been dreaming the same dreams I had—to play for their favorite team in "the show." Young ladies stared at the ballplayers, loving the game and the men who played it, hoping for an autograph and maybe more. The mainstay fans were there as well, the older couple who'd been coming there for every home game over the past however-many years. Suddenly, at that very moment, I realized what we had been fighting for—in that stadium and on that field was the tapestry of American life and the living examples of the freedoms we enjoy and often take for granted.

As Frank began snapping photos, I watched batting practice anxiously, wanting to grab my uniform and join them. I tried to enjoy the moment for what it was, but getting that close again made me nervous and happy at the same time. I didn't realize that I was about to enjoy one of my most memorable baseball experiences.

After Frank finished his photos, he suggested that we go up to the press box, and he took that occasion to reintroduce me to many of the sportswriters whom I'd known in years past. They weren't bothered by our interruption, and they were pleased to see me again. Frank escorted me to the executive boxes, where I said hello to Walter O'Malley, the legendary owner of the Dodgers who'd heeded Horace Greeley's words from years earlier: "Go west, young man, go west!" Although he had a very successful franchise in Brooklyn, the Dodgers were forever in the shadow of the Yankees. Perhaps O'Malley realized that he could maximize his team's potential by transporting them to L.A. He believed that he could set attendance records immediately, and he was right. Over 90,000 fans attended the October 6, 1959, World Series game in which the Dodgers hosted the Chicago White Sox—the largest single World Series crowd in history. O'Malley succeeded in opening baseball to the entire nation, and he's credited with bringing baseball to the West Coast, truly making it a "national pastime." Although many Brooklyn fans were disgruntled by the transition, O'Malley had solidified his legend, and the Dodgers were in Los Angeles to stay.

Shortly after speaking with Walter, I ran into Buzzie Bavasi, and he was as pleased as anyone to see me.

"I want to thank you for not forgetting me, Buzzie. Those packages were very important to me."

"Hey, Roy, it's the least I could do—once a Dodger, always a Dodger. Why don't you and Frank join me in the executive box for dinner before the game?"

We accepted, of course, and chatted about old times as we enjoyed the first-class service and great food. After finishing, we returned to our box seats high above the field as the announcer asked everyone to stand for the national anthem. As the song began, I flashed back to the jungles, and with the words, ". . . rocket's red glare," I remember the sounds and sights of war, the sound of RPGs, the screams of pain from the wounded and dying. I fought tears and emotions as the anthem concluded and our flag waved gently in the breeze.

I couldn't believe how fortunate I was to be back at Dodger Stadium, my church—my holy ground. Its beauty was so far removed from the mud and blood of the rice paddies I'd waded through for eight months, half a world away. But our men were still fighting and dying,

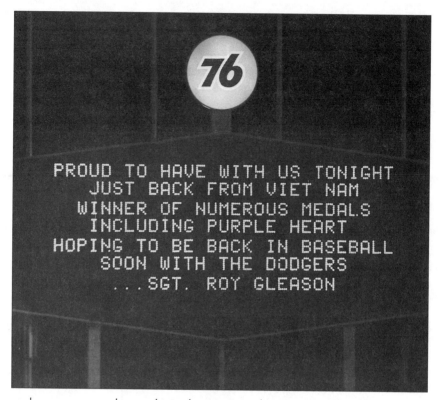

PROUD TO HAVE WITH US TONIGHT
JUST BACK FROM VIET NAM
WINNER OF NUMEROUS MEDALS
INCLUDING PURPLE HEART
HOPING TO BE BACK IN BASEBALL
SOON WITH THE DODGERS
...SGT. ROY GLEASON

At home on a convalescent leave during September 1968, Roy received a standing ovation when this message was broadcast at Dodger Stadium.

and that struck me fast as the song ended. Although I'm sure I radiated that sentiment, Frank nor anyone else said anything, and after a few minutes, my mind returned to the game I loved.

Unfortunately, I don't recall the particulars of the game that evening, most likely because I was in shock. I was finally back where I belonged, and I had trouble reminding myself of that. Attending that game was truly the "best medicine" that Dr. Frank could prescribe.

Sometime in the middle of the game, John Ramsey, the field announcer, made the broadcast to the packed stadium: "The Dodgers and the nation are proud to have with us tonight Roy Gleason, who has just returned from his tour of duty in Vietnam."

With that, they flashed my name across the scoreboard, and everyone around me—Frank, the Dodger brass, the sportswriters, and the commentators—asked me to stand and acknowledge the fans, who were giving me a standing ovation. I was stunned—I had no idea that this would happen, and the emotions were overwhelming. Although I was standing to recognize the fans, they really were recognizing all of us who went to Vietnam. They were acknowledging Tony Sivo and the others who gave their lives in a war that our leaders didn't seem to want to win. I was proud to represent those who died and those who were still fighting, even if only for a few moments.

I'm pretty shy, so I'm a bit skittish around crowds, and I remember feeling a bit embarrassed standing there in front of everyone. Why were they singling me out? I was no different than those who were fighting and dying. I was no hero. I sure as hell didn't ask to go. In fact, I did everything I could to keep from going. All of these thoughts contributed to my discomfort, but that moment stands far above any other baseball moment that I've experienced. I acknowledged the fans and did so with the thought of representing all of those who have served our nation.

The magic and energy of that night will never leave me. I knew that Tony Sivo, our officers, Staff Sergeant Long, PFC Harton, Gordan Clapp, and everyone I had served with were standing with me, pleased to know that our country remembered their sacrifices.

Frank pointed out something that I'll never forget. "Roy, what happened tonight at Dodger Stadium has nothing to do with baseball." You may not like it or believe it, but you and those who are fighting and dying in this insanity are truly heroes to most Americans, and that's much bigger and more important than baseball.

As his words and the fans' recognition echoed in my mind and faded into the evening, I realized that he was right, and something else he said hit home even harder.

"Roy, the best medicine for you is to never give up on your dream. You need to work hard at your therapy so you can get better. Then, even though I think you could have a great career in films and television, you need to return to baseball—stronger and better than ever. That's where your heart is."

"Thanks, Frank—thanks for everything. I am going to come back. I have only one mission now, and that's to play for the Dodgers in '69."

17

Returning to Baseball

Spring training began the same time it did every year, February, and I was there in '69. My discharge papers arrived a month earlier, and my war injuries had healed. My world had changed drastically, as had the world around me. America had elected a new president, Richard Nixon, who defeated Hubert Humphrey in a tight race, promising that he'd end the war ". . . with honor" and heal our scarred nation. Whether or not he fulfilled that promise is your call. Although I'd been released from the service officially, I still followed the situation in Vietnam closely. People I knew well were still fighting and dying. The North Vietnamese chose February of '69 to launch another attack similar to the Tet Offensive, besieging 100 South Vietnamese cities in battles that lasted through July.

But my world was Vietnam no more. That nightmare had ended, so I returned my attention to baseball and the fulfillment of my dream. The entire Dodgers organization, from the offices to the outfield, knew how poorly the team had played over the past two seasons. Everyone was saying that the team needed to rebuild—that they needed "new blood." Although I'd left plenty on the battlefield, I still had some fresh blood pumping through my veins—but I had to prove it on the ball field, where it counted.

The National League had expanded once again, this time to 12 teams as they added the San Diego Padres and the Montreal Expos. Major League Baseball was inviting its neighbors to join its national pastime—San Diego would invite many Latin-Americans to accept a team as their own, and Montreal spread the word to Canada. The American League followed suit, adding the Kansas City Royals, and the Seattle Pilots, which moved to Milwaukee a year later. As a result of the expansion, each league formed two separate divisions in order to play a League Championship Series for the pennant. The LCS would be the best of five games. I thought that this change would enable more teams to be contenders, and it increased the fans' excitement and hope throughout the season. The expansion also opened more doors for me in spring training, and I knew that this was exactly the break I needed to return to the show. I'd have to have the best spring I'd ever had to play again, though. I hadn't seen the show in six years, and I'd be 26 soon enough. After losing two seasons in Vietnam, I knew that the spring would make or break my career.

I prepared myself mentally and physically for whatever was thrown at me. I was a bit thin, but I was in the best shape of my life. The organization seemed happy to have me back, and even Walter Alston acknowledged my presence (although he still wasn't encouraging me in any way). Hopefully, that would change once I got onto the field.

॰ ॰ ॰

I reported on February 20, 1969, with the feeling that right field was my door back into the big leagues. Andy Kosco was my main competition—he was solid, too: four years of major-league experience, coming off a .240, 15-homer season with the Yankees. His experience gave him the edge, though, and my minor-league success wasn't going to be enough. I'd have to be great, and it was now or never. I took that motivation and used it to hit between .350 and .400. I was leading the team in the Triple Crown categories (batting average, home runs, and RBIs) as spring training ended, and I knew my

Spring training in Vero Beach, 1969—Roy's first year back from Vietnam.

Roy bats during spring training in 1969.

performance should have erased all doubts about my abilities and condition.

In the back of my mind, I wondered and hoped that Alston had forgotten about the bat-wrestling incident and remembered that I still had a hit in my only at-bat in the show. I sat in the locker room, eagerly awaiting the "great news. . . ."

Tommy Lasorda, who I knew well and respected, was given the dubious distinction of bearing that "news." Tommy was not yet a coach on Alston's staff, but he'd later become the Hall of Fame manager of the Dodgers, and he had a unique gift for wrapping bad news in positive paper. After all, he'd been through it himself. He was around 26 when Sandy Koufax had replaced him on the Dodgers' pitching staff 13 years earlier. I could tell when he walked into the room that the news wasn't going to be good. He pointed out that the Dodgers were very impressed with my performance, and they were amazed that I'd recovered so quickly. No one thought that I could do it, and they felt it was both miraculous and remarkable.

But. . . .

There was always a "but. . . ."

"Since you've missed the last two seasons, they feel that you'd be better off playing at Triple A-Albuquerque. You'll be playing every day, and you can get back into the routine of playing ball rather than sitting the bench in the show," Tommy explained.

Although he made it seem like the best decision for me, I was still devastated. What I wanted to ask him, but didn't, was, "How many times do I have to 'prove myself' to the Dodgers?" I played hard in '63 and played perfectly. Then, the Dodgers convinced me not to join the National Guard, even though they told many others to—and look where that got me. Now, after risking my life for my country, they were denying me the chance that they helped take away in the first place. I was their best hitter in the spring, and that wasn't enough for a chance?

Who the hell do they think they're kidding? I wasn't a kid anymore and was completely frusterated.

I went to Albuquerque, and while I started off doing well, I became more and more depressed about my future as the season progressed, and soon I was playing in Bakersfield (California League Class A). Recently, Ron Cey reminded me of playing together in Bakersfield— he remembered a game in which I pitched seven innings and hit home runs from both sides of the plate. By the end of the '69 season, even that bright spot couldn't change the fact that I was completely demoralized and devastated.

⤳ ⤳ ⤳

While I was at my lowest point, America was at its highest as Neil Armstrong became the first man to set foot on the moon on July 20, 1969. I was one of the 600 million people watching him on television, and I felt enormous pride for my country. As President Nixon said, "For one priceless moment in the history of man, the people of this Earth are truly one." As Apollo XI parachuted safely into the Pacific Ocean on July 24, 1969, I became lost in the sun's reflection, transported back a year in time—to the moment in which I was flying through the air, wounded, bloodied, but alive in the mud of Vietnam, staring into the blinding, partially-shaded sun.

On that day, I was sitting on the bench during a game, reflecting upon all that'd happened, remembering those I served with and those whom no one would see again. While President Kennedy's dream of placing a man on the moon had been realized, my dream was fading before my eyes, and I felt as far away from the game I loved as I did in the muddy jungle.

My family and friends seemed to share my pain, but perhaps I was just feeling sorry for myself. I was so discouraged, but my mother and others kept reassuring me, persuading me not to quit. I just couldn't understand why my dream was collapsing before my eyes. I hadn't survived a brutal war to sit the bench in Class A—I'd been through hell, and all I asked for was the chance. Why didn't they trade me if they thought that I couldn't help them? I didn't feel that they "owed" me the shot, but I thought I deserved a "fair" shot, and that had been taken from me.

Obviously, my perspective is biased due to my commitment to recover and get to the point where I could get my shot. Life isn't fair, though—look at Tony Sivo, our officers, and all the men lost in Vietnam. I was angry with the Dodgers, with my life, with myself, and I felt like all the effort and dedication toward my dream was for nothing.

Without the excuse of my injuries, 1969 was still my least successful season. I can only blame my performance on my loss of hope, determination, and confidence. I was missing the fire in my belly, and I felt like I was simply going through the motions. The passion was gone, and I'd changed.

Around that time, my niece, Reneé, first pointed out my apparent sadness. Children can see through the facades we show adults, and she saw into my soul.

None of this mattered to the Dodgers, who surely felt justified in sending me to the minors since I played poorly, and Andy Kosco posted career bests in right field. The Dodgers took fourth place in their division, eight games behind Atlanta. Due to damage in his right shoulder, Don Drysdale retired, leaving a huge void in the pitching staff. Fate had struck us both hard—Don had to leave the game he loved, and I was on my way to minor-league oblivion.

I truly didn't know if baseball was going to work for me—my future in baseball was turning into nothing but a dream. I didn't have anything else, though—just a high-school education and no real qualifications. I heard Frank Worth's words in my head, "Roy, you need to come back to baseball—that's where your heart is."

For the first time, I wondered if that was true.

18

A Chance for Redemption

A fter the '69 season, I was ready for something new, and that opportunity came as I was drafted by a young expansion team, the California Angels. The Dodgers sold my contract, and I'd been given a breath of fresh air as far as my career was concerned. All of this was due to one person—the same person who'd given me my first chance—Kenny Myers. He knew that I was unhappy, and since he'd left the Dodgers, he was instrumental in acquiring my contract for the Angels.

"Once a Dodger, always a Dodger," as Buzzie Bavasi had said, was no longer true, and that disappointed me. Yet I was unable to contribute to the team, and although I thought of the organization as family, I have to admit, at the time, I was happy to go elsewhere.

Joining the Angels left me nervous, though. What were they looking for? Would I get along with the manager (although I'd known him for years)? With the coaching staff? When did their spring training begin? How would I adjust to the team? Could I really make the team as a 27-year-old rookie? What did they need and could I help? How did the American League differ from the National League?

I'd followed the Angels since their inception in '60, when Gene Autry founded the franchise. They'd offered me the $100,000 bonus that I'd turned down for the Dodgers. In '61, they were known as the

Los Angeles Angels, and they played their home games at Wrigley Field in Los Angeles. They finished as most expansion teams did—near the bottom of the standings, 38 1/2 games out of first place. Since then, they'd ascended into a respectable team. In '62, when Dodger Stadium was opened, the Angels split the facilities with the Dodgers, and they jumped to third place, just 10 games out of first. Their young, outstanding pitching staff was led by Bo Belinsky, who pitched the Angels' first no-hitter in franchise history against the Orioles—who ironically had drafted Bo just a year earlier.

After sub-par seasons in '63 and '64, the Angels changed their name to the "California Angels" in '65, but faired no better, finishing in seventh place. That same season, the Twins lost to the Dodgers in the World Series, and Minnesota had come into the league with the Angels—which gave the franchise hope. By '66, the Angels had moved into the newly built Anaheim Stadium. Some local Native-American tribes protested the location, saying that an ancient burial ground was there, and they put a curse on the new facility. Only time would tell if the curse would prevail. They finished in sixth place, but only 18 games out of first, and few people remembered the hex.

After a decent showing in '67, the Angels were back near the bottom in '68. By '69, they showed promise, and the addition of new franchises thinned their competition. They finished in third place, but 26 games behind Minnesota and 20 games below .500. Ironically, the Angels experienced something that had never happened before in 1969. They fired their manager of eight years, Bill Rigney, replacing him in the middle of his ninth season with the club. The following season, he accepted the manager's position with the Twins and took them to another division championship.

The Angels replaced Bill with Harold "Lefty" Phillips, a former minor leaguer, scout, and coach from the Dodgers. I'd known Lefty for years, and although I didn't see him as a successful manager, his winning percentage with the Angels was .013 higher than Rigney's.

All that really set the scene for me in my eyes. I knew that the Angels hadn't been successful; I knew the manager well, and I believed he'd give me a fair shot—my chance at redemption. By January, 1970, I truly felt that I could help the ball club.

When I became an Angel, they were playing less than two miles from where I grew up in Garden Grove. I laugh when I say, ". . . I became an Angel," because my mother never considered me an angel, that's for sure.

Spring training didn't go the way I'd planned, as I was directed to the minor league training grounds instead of reporting with the major-league squad to Palm Springs. I went to Holtsville, which is in the California desert near the Mexican border. I realized that my performance was so poor from the year before that I'd have to reinvent myself, but the experience was like nothing I'd ever seen. The facilities were spartan, and the food was a joke—I had better grub in the jungles of Vietnam! We'd stand in long lines with cafeteria trays and receive a bowl of something that looked like beef stew along with an apple and some juice. We were miserable and hot each day, and the training lacked organization. I could see why the Angels were near the bottom of their division each year. Unlike the Dodgers, who'd built their organization on solid minor league clubs, the Angels seemed to go through the motions and little more. The neighboring franchises couldn't have been more night and day.

My field performance was decent during spring training, and I was even allowed to pitch some games, which the Dodgers rarely let me do. I really thought Lefty would call me up, especially after he'd see me in camp and go out of his way to acknowledge my service in the war. After spring training, though, I was optioned to Guadalajara in the Mexican League for the season. I'd made it back to the show, but it was the Mexican show, which was the equivalent of Triple-A ball here.

Of course, playing in Mexico was a trip. I didn't know any Spanish before going, and I didn't know what to expect. However, the crowds for each game were far larger than minor league games at home. I even earned a nickname from the league's official magazine after breaking out to a great start: "El Atomico," or "the atomic man."

By the end of 1970, I had a reinvigorated confidence, and although I was 27, I still believed that I had 10-12 years of play left in me. I was in a young, hungry organization, and I was willing to do whatever it was going to take. Whether you play baseball or not, everyone knows that it's difficult to keep your eye on the ball when you're staring into the sun.

19

A Dream Deferred

by Wallace Wasinack

As he extended his huge right hand professionally, he introduced himself, "Hi, my name is Roy. What's your name, and how can I help you?"

"I'm Wally, and I'm looking to lease a new car," I said.

"What are some things that you're looking for in a new car, Wally?" Roy reached into his pocket, and handed me his business card.

As I studied the name, I couldn't help thinking that it looked familiar. "Did you happen to go to Garden Grove High School?" I asked.

A bit surprised, he smiled and replied, "Yes. . . ."

"Did you play baseball there?"

He nodded with a grin, studying me.

"I'm sorry to ask so many questions, but I'm a former high school teacher. I think I remember you. . . . What year did you graduate?"

"In 1961," he said.

"I graduated from Garden Grove in 1957, and I played baseball, too."

His eyes lit up, and he said, "After graduating, I played professionally for a stint."

"Really? I think I do remember you. Do you know Kenny Myers?"

With a laugh, Roy said, "Kenny signed me. How do you know Kenny?"

"I played on the first Dodger Rookie team in '58, and Kenny was one of the coaches. Willie Davis was on the same team, and Kenny had just signed him out of school as well."

"I actually played two years on the Rookies as well—1960 and '61."

As I test drove the car (which I ultimately leased), we continued to dig through the past, and perhaps my experience as a teacher led me to ask many questions. Roy's story fascinated me, and I became more riveted with each answer.

"Have you ever considered writing a book about your life?" I asked him.

"From time to time, I guess," he said. "But I'm not a writer, and I haven't really done anything that great."

"I think you've done amazing things. You're a hero in my mind."

After some persuasion, I convinced him to work with me to tell his story, under one condition—that we found answers to the questions that had plagued him for over 30 years. Roy encouraged me to interview family members, close friends, former players and teammates, schoolmates, coaches, managers, veterans, and anyone else who could contribute to this tale.

Throughout my interviews, one question formed in my mind: "Why?"

Why had all these unfortunate circumstances fallen upon one man? Was it simply bad luck? Was it simply coincidence? Why did this man feel that much of his life was a disappointing failure?

Due to my baseball experience, I couldn't help asking questions such as, "Why didn't the Dodgers use him after he showed excellent skill as an outfielder?" A minor league Gold-Glove winner, Roy had Willie Davis's speed and a cannon for an arm. And after a double in his only at-bat, why was he never called upon to hit again?

Whatever the answers to those questions were, a bigger one remained.

Why was Roy Gleason the only draft-eligible young man from a major league team to go to Vietnam?

Roy wasn't protected like other Dodgers in this specific demographic. When he showed me a 1978 article from the *Chicago Sun-Times* entitled "Honor Men We Try to Forget," by Bill Gleason (no relation), it furthered my interest in his story. On our search to uncover answers, we unearthed information that will surprise and confuse you, and we allow you to draw your own conclusions.

The final question may be the most intriguing: "What happened to Roy Gleason after the 1970 season?"

"Irony" is generally defined as: "results that are the opposite of what was expected." Roy's life should be the diagram next to the definition.

Between the 1970 and 1971 seasons, Roy still felt that he had solid chances to play in the show, and he was more confident than ever. Many major leaguers had played all-star seasons well beyond Roy's 27 years, and his performance in the Mexican League had received praise from the organization. He took an off-season job doing construction in the California Mountains, hoping that the labor would keep him in shape as he paid the bills. At the end of one work day, he and a coworker were returning from the site in a truck when a boulder rolled into their path. Roy was in the passenger seat as the truck swerved and careened down the mountainside, flipping several times before coming to a halt. They dragged themselves from the vehicle, fearing an explosion, and Roy suddenly felt intense pain in his right shoulder and arm.

A doctor delivered the tragic news in the emergency room: Roy's rotator cuff was badly damaged, and he required major surgery.

"Will I be able to throw?" Roy asked hopefully.

"Even with immediate surgery, it would be extremely unlikely," the doctor told him.

Facing no other options, Roy went ahead with the procedure. As he lay upon that operating table, he couldn't help asking, "Why? Why, when everything was going so well again does this happen?"

The irony: The battlefield didn't end his career—a boulder did. His dream was snatched from him at 27 years old. Still, Roy didn't give up hope. He worked hard to prove the doctors wrong, got to a point where his abilities returned, and then re-injured his arm.

After years of various jobs outside of baseball, Dodger great Don Drysdale, who needed a bartender for his nightclub, offered Roy a position.

"Roy, I'm looking for someone I can trust—someone without glue on his fingers," Roy recalls Don telling him.

Roy accepted and enjoyed the opportunity to see old friends.

"You were a real-life Sam Malone," I told him, thinking of the character from *Cheers*.

During this period, Roy met and married his first wife, Donna.

"The marriage was a disaster from day one," he said. "It was so bad that I asked the army recruiting office to send me as far away as they could."

They obliged, and Roy was sent to a strategic location in Greece, overseeing nuclear warheads. He was divorced shortly thereafter.

By 1982, Roy was back in the States and remarried to Sharron Von Brandis, a former tennis star from South Africa. Although they divorced in 1994, they had two sons, Troy and Kaile.

When I interviewed Roy's sons, I found that they were very supportive of his life, and they knew he expected great things from them. They didn't know much about Roy's baseball career, and I understood that Vietnam was a difficult subject for them to broach as well. Each had a very different outlook, though, as people always do. Troy was quiet and intelligent, subtly witty, and focused on his future (racing cars). Kaile, the youngest, was very expressive, and although very intelligent as well, saw himself as a writer in his future. Perhaps this story will serve as a springboard for both boys to aim for unparalleled heights.

Since their mother was a tennis player, I wondered what sports the boys played, but Roy informed me that Troy prefers fast cars to fastballs, and Kaile's six-foot-four frame led him to the free-throw line instead of the batter's box.

I also had the opportunity to speak with Roy's mother, Molly, who was living in a convalescent home. Although she lit up when asked about

Roy with his mother, Molly, in 1992. *From the Roy Gleason Collection*

her son, she was very guarded in her comments about the Dodgers and Vietnam, saying, "My son was never given a fair chance."

While playing for Duke Snider in the Northwest League during the '66 season, Roy learned that his niece, Karin, had been hit by a car. An airline strike at the time forced him to turn to the Dodgers, who flew him home immediately, but he learned that his three-year-old niece had died from the injuries. Through the grief, Roy pressed on further in his career with her angel on his shoulder.

If that doesn't tell you enough about Roy's character, this will:

After a night on the town, Roy and Wazy Wasdyke decided to have a late-night, early-morning breakfast at a local diner. After sitting in a booth, they noticed three young ladies in an adjacent booth, and the girls asked the two to join them. A short while later, one of the ladies' husbands came into the diner. After saying something to her, as she was sitting next to Roy, the man pulled out a gun and held it to Roy's cheek. The girls screamed, and the manager phoned the police. Roy stood, gun to his cheek, and grabbed a table knife.

"I'm going to pull the trigger, woman!" The gunman shouted to his wife.

"I don't even know him! We just met! We're just having breakfast!" She blurted truthfully.

Roy turned to the man, looked him straight in the eye, and with the gun still at his face, he said, "You don't have the balls to pull that trigger. . . ."

The man's eyes widened, and Wazy poked his head into view. "If I were you, I wouldn't mess with him. He just returned from Vietnam. Besides, if you fire, you'll mess up all of our food."

The gunman sensed Roy's fearlessness, stepped back, put the gun in his pocket, and quickly exited the diner. The man was apprehended in the parking lot by the police. The radio became the soundtrack for the scene, and after a few moments, everything was back to normal. They sat down, finished their meals, and the manager informed them that everything was "on the house."

That story not only proves Roy's courage in the face of adversity, but his yearning to live a normal life after an experience that was closer to hell than reality.

Before closing my research, I decided to contact the Dodgers to see if they could contribute anything to the book, and I was directed to Mark Langill, their official historian. That call led to an amazing moment, one that changed Roy's life forever and solidified this tale of missed opportunities, denied dreams, courage, heroism, and redemption.

Afterword

by Mark Langill

Publications Editor and Team Historian
for the Los Angeles Dodgers

There is a wide range of possible requests from people who call the publications office at Dodger Stadium. And because Dodger baseball touches so many generations, requests can came from a retired fan wanting a television schedule to a grade-school student working on a book report, looking for information.

Wally Wasinack's phone message in July of 2003 was a typical inquiry about a former Dodger. Our office also administers the team's Alumni Association and keeps in touch with more than 400 former Brooklyn and Los Angeles players through an annual questionnaire and in-house newsletter. Many authors use this Association as a vehicle to contact former ballplayers for interview requests.

When I called Wally, he asked if I knew of Roy's background. In the baseball record book, his line from 1963 is the bare-bones bottom line of so many players who had a "cup of coffee" with a major league team—a nice way of describing one's brief career.

I knew Roy's name and statistics from the record book, but I was intrigued when Wally began to recite this former Dodger's background, including receiving the Purple Heart. Our Alumni Association files didn't have a current address on Roy, but Wally mentioned that the former player might be living somewhere in Orange County.

This phone call was the beginning of a unique alliance with Wally, a businessman whose interest in Roy's career led to a friendship and journalistic journey that included the lush green playing field of Dodger Stadium and the unimaginable horror of war.

There are photo files at the ballpark that stretch back to the 1940s and 1950s, and the thick Roy Gleason folder remained intact when located in the archives. There were photos of Roy's graduation in 1961, posing with his family and scout Kenny Myers. There were also standard mug shots, bat-on-shoulder poses, and other "glamour" shots from the early years of Roy's career. The only indication of Roy's war accomplishments was one newspaper clipping from Los Angeles *Herald-Examiner* columnist Bob Hunter, whose 1969 spring training feature focused on Roy's comeback attempt from the numerous shrapnel injuries suffered in Vietnam.

I invited Wally to visit the ballpark, and he mentioned he might bring along Roy. When I met Roy and Wally on the morning of July 17, 2003, they were a contrast in personalities. The budding author was filled with enthusiasm, ideas, and questions about Dodger baseball and Roy's career. The ballplayer, although very polite, was quiet and reserved. I couldn't quite tell what was going through his mind as he roamed the ballpark for the first time in 20 years. But his chiseled six-foot-five frame indicated this former athlete could still tear a telephone book in half without flinching.

We retreated to a luxury box on the Club Level and reviewed the photographs. Wally spent more time offering tidbits from Roy's life, ranging from his youth league days to his time on the Hollywood soundstages. Roy wasn't listening to Wally's stories, or was he? Sometimes, Roy seemed to disappear in the moment, whether looking at photos or spotting something familiar on the stadium tour. He marveled at the new features at Dodger Stadium—both in the structure of the ballpark and its playing field. But he looked at the maze of ceiling pipes along the clubhouse hallways as an old friend because it hadn't changed in 40 years.

During the visit, Roy mentioned that his bats and uniforms were in the car. He returned with a 36-inch, 36-ounce Louisville Slugger with his flowing cursive signature branded into the bat's barrel. The uniforms were his home and road jersey tops, flannel treasures preserved in a dry cleaning bag. Along the bottom of the shirttail were the stitched words "Gleason, 1963"—the watermark of an authentic Dodger uniform produced by Goodman and Sons manufacturers in Los Angeles. Roy slipped on the uniform and posed for photos on the field with his bat. He hadn't worn the jersey in more than two decades, yet he didn't seem self-conscious wearing it on the playing field. He even fiddled with the grip of his bat and took a few soft swings into the air.

The most poignant moment occurred moments after we left the playing field. There are two walls bordering a narrow walkway leading from the dugout club restaurant to the elevators. One wall is a timeline of Dodger history since 1890. The other wall contains virtually every name of current and former Los Angeles and Brooklyn Dodgers who played in the 19th and 20th centuries.

Roy glanced at the wall, assuming his name wouldn't be there. I encouraged him to look anyway, but the seconds seemed like minutes, and I couldn't be sure his name was there. "Please be up there. Please be up there," I thought impatiently. Roy found his name and was pleasantly surprised. It was perhaps the first tangible sign that although he had been away for so long, his accomplishments were not forgotten by the Dodgers. He looked at the wall in a different context, glancing at the names around his, including Hall-of-Famer Roy Campanella.

But I realized there would always be two sides to the story with Roy Gleason. As he stood in front of the collage of names, the Vietnam veteran quietly said, "I'd rather be on this wall than the other one."

At that point, I realized Roy's story should be told in *Dodger Magazine*. At the very least, we could chronicle his life and celebrate the 40th anniversary of his major league debut for the September issue.

There was more to the story, though. During our interview in the luxury suite, Roy narrated his life with photos in a small scrapbook, a modest collection of snapshots and newspaper clippings. There was a photo of a military ceremony as the soldier standing at attention received his sergeant stripes from two military officials. Roy pointed to a watch on his left wrist and said the watch shattered when he was struck by enemy fire during an ambush on July 24, 1968. He also mentioned how he lost the belongings from his footlocker while being transported to the hospital, including his mother's wedding ring and a Dodger World Series ring. He didn't dwell on the Dodger ring, calling it "long gone" with a shrug of his shoulders.

A light bulb went off in my head—I wanted Roy to have a World Series ring. You can't put a Band-Aid on a man's life and pretend the past 30 years of heartache and disappointment never happened. But a championship ring is the ultimate prize in sports, and restoring his seemed appropriate. Roy Gleason didn't ask the Dodgers for anything. It was obvious this was a man of character and somehow this former talented but immature athlete had blossomed into a real-life patriot.

"You never know what's going to happen when the enemy begins shooting," Roy told me in a hushed but firm tone. "Are you going to run away? I didn't run."

Roy attended an afternoon game at Dodger Stadium a few days later and enjoyed a surprise reunion with National League umpire Bruce Froemming. When he was reintroduced to Roy, Froemming exclaimed, "Northwest League, 1962. . . . " like an excited game show contestant, and began the first of many minor league stories to the delight of the stunned subject.

After the baseball stories ended, Froemming discussed his own military obligations and how his reserve unit was nearly activated. When informed Gleason had received a Purple Heart, Froemming pressed him for information. But unlike his baseball stories, Roy spared him detailed descriptions. Froemming recalled how a relative was nearly killed in the Korean War, and how he still couldn't understand why the enemy soldier backed off and let the man escape instead of shooting him at pointblank range.

Roy Gleason with Bruce Froemming. *Photo by Mark Langill*

September 21, 2003—Roy with Vin Scully on the *Dodger Dugout* show.

"War is hell, there's no other way you can describe it," Froemming said. "But sometimes, there are good stories that emerge—not often, but sometimes."

Gleason nodded without comment.

The next day, I approached Derrick Hall, the former Dodgers vice president of communications, with an idea to honor Roy at the ballpark and present him with a World Series ring. I suggested our final home series in September with the San Francisco Giants because of the expected sellout crowds. Derrick gave his blessing, which triggered an exciting chain of events that would exceed my own hopes and expectations.

I ordered a new ring through Phyllis Moats, a member of the Human Resources department, who processes any request involving replacement World Series rings. Phyllis called the Balfour Company in

Texas and learned they would have to research the original design of the Dodgers' 1963 ring.

The *Dodger Magazine* feature ran five pages and received positive comments at the stadium. During this time, I approached Rob Menschel, a television cameraman and producer of the *Dodger Dugout* pregame show. Although he had the services of Hall of Fame broadcaster Vin Scully, Rob was driven to find unique stories, and he often went to great lengths to research historical events such as the 1959 World Series and the origin of the Dodgers and Angels rivalry in Southern California when the two teams shared Dodger Stadium from 1962-65.

I figured Roy might be a perfect segment for one of Rob's shows, and he immediately was interested. He approached Scully about Gleason's story and was told of the World Series ring being replaced in some manner. Scully agreed to conduct an interview, but this would be under special circumstances. Scully has been with the Dodgers since 1950 and he witnessed the Gleason career firsthand.

"He was one of those guys who could do everything," Scully told Rob in the press box. "He even looked good coming off the plane."

Scully also served in the Navy in World War II, and he was sensitive to a veteran's feelings and flashbacks. During the first week in September, Gleason met Scully in the dugout club and conducted a heartfelt interview for more than a half hour. I don't think anyone else could've pulled such feeling from Roy's soul, but the ballplayer later explained, "It was like talking to an old friend."

The impact of the interview was so powerful that Rob and Vin decided to devote the entire pregame show on September 21, 2003, to Roy's life.

But there was still the matter of Roy's on-field moment. He was under the assumption for weeks that the Dodgers only wanted him to throw out the ceremonial first pitch prior to the September 20 game. This was true, but it was only the tip of the iceberg. Scully suggested Roy receive his World Series ring on the field in front of the fans. A nice idea, but only Scully could suggest and execute such a bold move. It was decided that once Roy threw out the first pitch, Scully would tell Roy to stay on the field for a special presentation.

In the military, this would be classified as an ambush. But in baseball terms, this was a combination of both a surprise party and a show of appreciation for a man who impressed everyone he met. And the driving force behind these plans wasn't the thought of television ratings or positive publicity for the ball club. This was a challenge to give this man a special moment, something more than a World Series ring but a feeling of appreciation and gratitude for serving his country when it meant setting aside his own dreams.

Scully took a personal interest in this project, and he even told the secret plans to former Dodger outfielder Wally Moon over dinner when the ball club was in Houston in mid-September.

Meanwhile, Wally Wasinack had no idea what was happening. As the pipeline to Roy, it was better to leave him out of the loop. And so our frequent conversations centered on "the first pitch" and whether Roy would have enough juice left in his arm to throw the ball to the catcher without a bounce.

A few days before Roy's ceremony, *Los Angeles Times* columnist Bill Plaschke wrote a heartwarming story about Gleason's life and the upcoming ceremony. Bill knew about the ring, but he didn't reveal the secret in his story. Instead, he touched on Roy's military background, along with the hopes, dreams, and disappointments of his life. The front-page column also featured a large color photo of the modern-day Roy at Dodger Stadium with the pullout quote from his first visit in July, "I'm glad I'm on that wall, instead of the other wall."

Considered one of the country's top sports columnist, Plaschke tugged at the reader's heartstrings, and the response was overwhelming. The telephone rang off the hook that afternoon and everyone from writers to fans called to find out more information on Roy Gleason.

One of the callers was Margie Myers, the daughter of Dodger scout Kenny Myers, who hadn't attended a Dodger game for two decades. Margie had visited the ballpark one afternoon to reflect on her family's

September 20, 2003—Roy listens to Vin Scully's announcement about his military service and baseball career.

September 20, 2003—Roy with his sons, Troy and Kaile.

association with the Dodgers. When a security guard didn't recognize her father's name, she went back home and never returned. Now, with Roy Gleason back at Dodger Stadium, she wanted to purchase the best seats available and witness Roy's moment.

In the press box that evening, I saw co-conspirator Vin Scully walking toward the booth. We didn't even speak; instead exchanging winks as if a pail of water was about to fall on one of our unsuspecting friends. Rob announced his show was almost complete, and he would splice the added footage of the first pitch and ring ceremonies into the segment following Roy's interview with Scully. Rob devoted a great amount of time to the production, even driving at 5:00 a.m. from the San Fernando Valley to interview former Dodger general manager Buzzie Bavasi at his La Jolla home.

September 20, 2003—Roy throws out the first pitch.

Keeping the ring safe was another challenge. It arrived from Human Resources on a Thursday, which meant carrying it wherever I went for the next three days. It was even on the nightstand when I slept, which grew harder and harder as the big event approached.

The quiet of a Saturday morning lasted only a few moments until I logged onto the computer for some sports news. This was a time for college football, Kobe Bryant and the major league pennant races. But imagine my shock when the lead story to the entire country was about Roy Gleason, "AFTER 40 YEARS, DODGER COMING HOME." The story paraphrased Plaschke's column and added quotes from the Dodgers about the upcoming game. I called Wally, but couldn't tell him I was amazed because people think he's just throwing out the first pitch. Instead, we agreed the first pitch would be exciting, and he assured me Roy and his guests would all be in place well before the start of batting practice.

Roy and his family arrived at Dodger Stadium around 5:00 p.m. He introduced the members of his extended family and then excused himself because he forgot the tickets in his car. His two sons, Troy and Kaile, his sister Kathy and her husband John and John's youngest son Michael, Roy's friends Paul and Marie Palmquist and Wally were eagerly looking forward to the game and the evening's festivities. We put everyone in a conference room on the club level because of the pregame production meetings in the press box.

Wally couldn't understand why I told him to give his video recorder to Roy's brother-in-law.

"You can stand on the field with me," I said.

At 6:15 p.m., I brought Margie Myers and her niece from the loge section to the conference room. The reunion was special, as Margie pulled a charm bracelet from her purse. Pointing to the different baseball medals, she said, "I know my father is here tonight."

At 6:30, I collected Kaile and Troy from the box seats where they were watching batting practice and escorted everyone toward the field. Any nervousness on my part went out the window thanks to Troy, who was chatting on his cell phone and speculating when he could get to a party later that night in San Diego. He explained there would be a "roomful of girls" in attendance and he would try to be there by 9:30.

Suddenly, the biggest challenge was how a baseball historian could convince a teenager to get off the phone. Scrambling for an official party line, I announced that National League rules prohibited the use of cell phones on the field because of concerns of gambling. He seemed puzzled when I explained the threat of "last-minute insider information," but he shrugged his shoulders, folded his phone, and tucked it back into his pocket.

Roy was expecting to throw out the first pitch around 6:50, and he seemed at ease during the 10 minutes we waited along the railing in front of the dugout club seats. Derrick Hall shook his hand as did Dodger photographer Jon SooHoo. As Roy put his arms around his sons for a photograph, the television cameraman filmed the scene,

ABOVE: September 20, 2003—Roy salutes the crowd.
BELOW: Roy receives his 1963 World Series ring from Dodger manager, Jim
Tracy.

Roy receives congratulations from the Dodgers and extends his thanks.

while Rob coordinated six different cameras in the ballpark from his headset in the broadcasting booth.

Pregame coordinator Elaine Lombardi found a baseball for Roy and he instinctively flipped it to himself a few times, spinning upward and snatching it. I escorted Roy to an area behind home plate at 6:48 and said, "You're supposed to face the scoreboard during the introduction."

I walked back to the group near the railing of the dugout seats; I leaned over to Wally and said, "There are a few things I forgot to tell you. . . ."

The video screen in left field played a two-minute message from Scully, which he had taped the previous afternoon. He outlined Roy's military and athletic accomplishments as images from Roy's life flashed on the screen.

For all our planning, nobody could predict Roy's reaction. He watched Scully's message on the giant video screen with an expressionless face and then shocked me by saluting the color guard and offered a solemn military salute to all sides of the ballpark. The ovation was thunderous, thanks in part to inflatable plastic sticks given away to fans on "Noisemaker Night." I usually hate those things when watching a ballgame in the grandstands, but I was thrilled to hear the crowd's enthusiasm, another unknown factor when planning.

Roy one-hopped the first pitch, and he smiled to himself as he walked toward catcher David Ross. Suddenly, Scully's booming voice cried out, "Hold it, Roy. . . . Hold it right there!" Roy looked toward the press box in a bewildered manner, searching for Scully amidst the bright lights and crowd.

It was the first time in Dodger Stadium history that Scully had participated in such a moment, so the fans weren't quite sure what would follow. Roy turned toward the third base dugout as Manager Jim Tracy and the Dodger players began walking toward the third-base line. Tracy extended his hand to Roy and presented the World Series ring. As the scene played out on the stadium's video screen in left field, I could see Roy mouth the words, "Hey, Jim," as the manager approached. Tracy shook hands with Roy and no doubt said something appropriate for the occasion. Roy looked bewildered but composed when he stood with Tracy and held the open ring box in his large hand like a tiny baseball.

As Roy walked along the third-base line, he eventually broke into a smile as the Dodger players shook his hand. Rookie Edwin Jackson, just 20 years old and a major leaguer for two weeks, was surprised when Roy patted his jersey and said, "That's my number."

Along the dugout seat railing, Kaile and Troy watched with obvious surprise, as their father became the center of the baseball universe for a few moments. Wally was speechless during this time, shaking his head with amazement as the fruits of his original idea played out.

"Aren't you glad you made that phone call?" I said, patting his shoulder.

It was now time for the national anthem, and Roy took his place alongside Tracy and the Dodgers. This was also a planned part of the program because of Roy's service to his country.

After the national anthem, Roy and Coach John Shelby stayed together on the field. Shelby once learned from Dodger infielder Dave Hansen that one isn't supposed to leave the field until the color guard departs. Gleason wasn't going to ignore this protocol, even under these unique circumstances, and he remained at attention with Shelby until the guard made their exit.

It was now time to prepare for the ballgame, and the pregame guests made their way to the grandstands. Our group left the buzz of the field and stepped into a quiet corridor leading toward the stairs for the other stadium levels.

The pressure was finally off, and I asked Roy with a surprised look, "Didn't I mention the ring?"

Everyone laughed and admired the piece of jewelry. I had guessed a size nine would be large enough, but it would only fit on Roy's pinkie finger. I offered to send it to the manufacturer to resize the ring, but Roy announced he wasn't going to let this one out of his sight.

When Roy stepped onto the escalator, fans traveling in the other direction offered their outstretched hands and offered their praise. There were autograph seekers, but also those who simply shook his hand.

The Dodger public relations department asked if Gleason would meet with reporters in the press box around 7:15. They retreated to the back dining room, and Roy held court with approximately 10 reporters and columnists, describing his emotions on the field and giving background on his life in baseball and the military.

Watching from about 10 feet away was Troy Gleason, back on the cell phone while his father answered questions from each of the reporters. Troy hung up the phone and laughed as he weighed two mythical packages in his outstretched palms. "Room full of girls, a priceless moment. . . . Room full of girls? A priceless moment."

Troy delayed leaving for his party long enough to watch the interviews and visit the private box of former Dodger Chairman Bob Daly, who wanted to extend his regards to Roy. Also in the box were several prominent major league officials, including Deputy Commissioner Sandy Alderson. One hour after his quiet reunion with Margie Myers, Roy was holding court in the owner's suite.

Roy eventually watched the game from aisle 15 behind the Dodger dugout. There was a steady stream of autograph-seekers and well-wishers. He appeared on the giant video screen in the seventh inning, singing "Take Me Out to the Ballgame." But there wasn't much time to savor the evening, because the Dodgers and Giants played a rather fast-paced game. Roy and his family returned to the press box in the bottom of the ninth inning as the Dodgers were losing 4-0.

Roy wanted to introduce his family to Vin Scully, but I advised that he was busy before the game, and this was a better time as everyone waited for the postgame traffic to subside. Scully was happily surprised to see Gleason in the dining room when he emerged from the broadcasting booth. They shared an embrace and Scully posed for pictures with everyone. Roy was at a loss of words when he tried to thank Scully for his role in the ceremony. Scully smiled and simply said, "You're welcome, Roy—anytime. . . . " as if the master could recreate the magic again on a moment's notice.

Next came Rob Menschel, the five-foot-three television producer who would be awake until 3:00 a.m. editing the ring ceremony footage into the next day's pregame show. Rob had always talked in general terms about the segment and didn't reveal the extent of the package, which included exhaustive research and footage on Roy's Hollywood appearances and the Vietnam War. Rob stood in front of the ballplayer and confessed with a schoolboy grin, outstretched arms and open palms of someone with no more secrets: "Now you know how the story ends!" he exclaimed as Roy wrapped his right arm around Rob's shoulders.

The party made its way into a deserted parking lot at 11:55 p.m. On the radio, broadcaster Ross Porter was playing an interview from

Tracy on his postgame Dodger talk show. The comments didn't focus on the ball game or the pennant race. Instead, Tracy recalled the pregame ceremonies with Gleason and how much it meant to be part of such a moment.

While walking with the Gleason family in the parking lot, I knew it was the end of an incredible journey. The glow of the stadium lights illuminated the lone vehicle in the parking lot, and we exchanged our farewells with the promise of everyone watching Rob's television show in the morning. That was one last surprise—the entire show was being devoted to Roy—but we kept that secret until the last moment because of potential pre-empting coverage of war or other natural disaster knocking him off the air.

The program ran in its entirety, although I couldn't watch it live because of the pregame activities of another ballgame. I watched the Roy Gleason story on television a few hours later in the privacy of my home, which turned out to be a wise decision. I finally cried.

Mark's words certainly captured the activity and the behind-the-scenes excitement that culminated on the weekend of September 20, 2003. As he indicated, I was totally blown away by the caring and thoughtfulness of Mark, Vin Scully, Rob Menschel, Derrick Hall, Bill Plaschke, and all of those who helped make this recognition so memorable.

Sometime later I caught up to Rob Menschel and asked about some of his thoughts regarding all that had occurred. In his most modest way, he said he had been very pleased to be a part of helping to tell Roy's story. He went on to say that he has a veteran production crew consisting of 25 people. He said that they have worked together for many years covering many sporting events. He said, "They pretty much have seen it all."

Normally, during a sports production, there is a certain amount of conversation among the crew. He said on the night Roy Gleason was recognized, he noticed that, "Everyone in the production crew remained totally silent, as if they had all recognized that this was indeed a very special recognition."

Epilogue
by Roy Gleason

W ally has asked me to tell you how I felt about my life, particularly over the last few months, so I'll try to be as honest as I can, and I hope that I can leave you with something meaningful and useful.

Before beginning this project more than four years ago, I felt my life was one of lost opportunities—full of guilt and regret. I felt that I did not live up to my own expectations, and all that I was truly proud of were my sons.

Although my marriage to their mother didn't work out, my sons knew that I loved them and still do. I would also do whatever I could or can to help them achieve their dreams. They knew my financial situation, so they never really asked for material things. They would call me from time to time, and they knew I would always be there for them, and that will never change. Although the marriage failed, I never felt I was a failure as a father, and I hope that my sons agree with that.

As we began this account, I thought my life wasn't very interesting, and it certainly lacked the "happy ending" that many people enjoy. I wanted to end the book with the fans' recognition I received in 1968 as I was recovering from my wounds. But that all changed when Wally called Mark.

It's difficult to describe my feelings on Saturday, September 20, 2003, at Dodger Stadium. I cannot thank all those in attendance for making it the most incredible moment of my life, and I'm so pleased that my sons, my family, and those who are dear to me were able to witness my joy. That moment felt like having the key to heaven in my pocket, and it was something that I wanted to hold on to forever.

As I walked out to throw the ceremonial first pitch, my spirit seemed to leave my body to observe, and I can't recall much of that particular moment. But reality returned when I short-hopped the ball to Dodger catcher, David Ross. As I walked off the field, somewhat embarrassed, a booming voice (Vin Scully) dropped upon me:

"Hold it, Roy! Hold it right there!"

For an instant, I thought it was God speaking to me. Lost in the stadium lights, I thought, "So, does God [Vin] want to redo the throw? I don't mind. . . . I'd take my jacket off and fire one in there, for old time's sake."

But Vin told me to look to the dugout, from where Dodger manager Jim Tracy was emerging ahead of the entire team. I was in shock when he handed me the World Series ring, and it remains one of the most incredible instants of my life. I felt like I was finally back to where I always wanted to be—I felt like I was 20 years old again, and the only regret I have now is that it couldn't continue.

Those moments are outweighed only by what happened next. As I stood at attention for the national anthem, emotion overwhelmed me, and I realized that the Dodgers and the fans were recognizing all those who have gone to war, fought, and sacrificed some part or all of their lives for us. I was merely a momentary figurehead for veterans from all wars, especially the thousands who perished in the jungles of Vietnam.

When our flag and colors were introduced, I instinctively saluted all those who never came home—from Tony Sivo to the men and women fighting today. I choked back the tears that carried 30 years of sacrificial blood that I'd witnessed, remembered, or bled, and I hoped that I could represent those men and women with honor. Those fans on their feet paid homage to those who were never recognized, who had gone without tribute until that night. That left it impossible to maintain my composure, and I sacrificed my poise to the moment.

Again, I was at a loss for words when Vin Scully devoted his entire *Dodger Dugout* pregame show the next day to my life. Although they described my career and experiences with the highest respect, I couldn't help feeling guilty that I was receiving something that hundreds of thousands of men and women before and after me deserved.

Sometime later, an article appeared in *Vietnam Veterans of America* magazine. Written by Michael Arkush, the piece documents my return to the Dodgers, touches upon my past, and mentions that this book was in the works. That article led me to many fellow servicemen who I knew from the war and from "Fort Courage." I heard from Paul Davis, who was stationed there with me, and learned that Paul was one of the men who helped clear the area the day I was wounded. He even helped get me onto the chopper. We spoke of others whom we missed and knew nothing about: First Sergeant Johnson, Hammerschmidt, and many others.

My life has been a rollercoaster of joy and pain, but where I was disappointed, I'm now filled with gratitude and appreciation. I do have one remaining goal, though: to return to professional baseball in some capacity. From scouting to coaching, I believe I can provide skills to help a team, and I'd love to give back to the game that has given me so much in my life. Baseball is a magical mistress, and even today, it continues to seduce me.

I will close by saying, simply, that forever I am indebted to all those who've recognized not what I have done, but what *we* did—what we sacrificed in those jungles, at that place no one wanted to go and many never left, where we were all lost in the sun.

Roy Gleason
"36"

National Association of Professional Baseball Leagues

INSTRUCTIONS: Use Box #1 <u>only</u> when player is transferred off active list because of suspension, temporary inactivity or disability. When player is reinstated make out new forms and use Box #2 <u>only</u>.

PRINT   OR   TYPE

MAIL ONE NOTICE **AT ONCE** TO:
(1) President National Association.
(2) President of your League.
(3) Hand one to player. (If not possible, mail copy to player by REGISTERED or CERTIFIED MAIL.)
(4) Retain one copy for your files.

Box No. 1

NOTICE TO PLAYER OF TRANSFER FROM ACTIVE LIST

...............April 13, 1967...............
(Date)

To Player......Roy William Gleason..

(Cross out terms which do not apply)
~~SUSPENDED~~
You are hereby officially notified of your placement upon the TEMPORARILY INACTIVE
~~DISABLED~~

list effective this ..13th..day of .....April................19..67. For a term of ...Indefinite.......

Reason ► Retu rned hom e, pending induction into military service

Inland Empire Baseball Club (Spokane..........Club .....Pacific Coast........League

By....*Elten Schiller*........................... General Manager
Elten Schiller   (Title)

- -

RECEIPT

....
(Date)

RECEIPT OF COPY OF THIS OFFICIAL NOTICE IS ACKNOWLEDGED
Certified Mail - Return Receipt Requested
to player #885571 - to N.A. #885572 .... Player

Place X in box if player is sent copy ►   [X] PLAYER SENT COPY OF THIS OFFICIAL NOTICE
by registered or certified mail.   BY REGISTERED OR CERTIFIED MAIL.

Box No. 2 ### NOTICE TO PLAYER OF REINSTATEMENT TO ACTIVE LIST

....
(Date)

To Player..

(Cross out terms which do not apply)
SUSPENDED
You are hereby notified of your reinstatement from TEMPORARILY INACTIVE list to the active
DISABLED
list this..........day of.................................... 19.......

.... Club .... League

By.. ....
(Title)

Printed in U. S. A. (10-65)

From the Roy Gleason Collection

LOS ANGELES DODGERS, INC.
1000 ELYSIAN PARK AVENUE
LOS ANGELES, CALIFORNIA 90012
TELEPHONE: 225-1411

July 18, 1967

Pvt. Roy Gleason
US 56704936
Co. A 5th Bn., 3rd Tng Bge.,
Fort Polk, La. 71459

Dear Roy:

Many thanks for your letter of July 16.

Send me the name of your company commander as quickly
as possible and where I should write to him. I would like
to try once more to see about getting you a "hardship case
release". There is no reason why you should go into hock
for the rest of your life for a needless situation.

Regards.

Very truly yours,

Buzzie

E. J. Bavasi

ew

Captain Michael B.
Patterson

LAKEVILLE BASEBALL CAMP, INC.

Area Code 617 947-0726   Lakeville, Mass. 02346

August 5, 1968

Sgt. Roy W. Gleason
U.S. 56704936
Co. A 3/39th Inf. 9th Div.
APO SF 96371

Dear Roy:

I received your letter and I sure do remember you as
the young fellow I met at the Stevenson's home in Los Angeles
and you were about ready to sign, I think, with the Dodges.

After reading your letter I certainly hope you get out
of that rat trap. It is a long run I can see by your letter
and it has done you a lot of good. I have to admit that my
service hitch straightened my thinking out a lot the same
way.

As to your line of thought on hitting I can only tell
you you have the right idea about trying to hold your weight
back until the last second and I agree completely that a
hitch is the most over-rated fault that people harp about
and your statement about your body balance is really a key
factor and what I'm trying to say is that in your standing
position, ready position and swinging position and follow-
through should all be in a balanced position. I won't get
in to too much of this as when you get back you can write
to me again and maybe some time we can get together and I
can have a personal chat with you.

I certainly wish you a lot of luck over there. Good luck.

Sincerely,

Ted Williams

TW:mfg